BIANCA ANDREESCU
SHE THE NORTH

Stephanie Myles

30 YEARS

TRIUMPH
BOOKS

This book is available in quantity at special
discounts for your group or organization.
For further information, contact:

Triumph Books LLC
814 North Franklin Street
Chicago, Illinois 60610
(312) 337-0747
www.triumphbooks.com

Printed in U.S.A.
ISBN: 978-1-62937-808-4
Design by Patricia Frey
Photos courtesy of the author unless
otherwise indicated.

INTRODUCTION

With 23 career Grand Slam titles and looking to put the all-time record of 24 out of reach, 37-year-old Serena Williams was trying to make tennis history in the 2019 US Open women's singles final.

Bianca Andreescu, who wasn't even born when Williams won her first US Open, *made history*—the first Canadian ever to win a Grand Slam singles title.

And she did it in her US Open main draw debut, something no other woman had ever done.

In triumph, the 19-year-old became an overnight sensation.

At No. 152 in the WTA rankings to start the season, the victory vaulted Andreescu all the way to No. 5 in the world.

She is tennis' new star—and the future of the game.

Andreescu's game style is unique in modern women's tennis. A potent mixture of power and determination partnered with improvisation and whimsy, she has turned the WTA Tour upside down.

And for the foreseeable future, the rest of the women will scramble to figure out ways to defeat a player who has so many different ways to win.

When Andreescu returned home to her native Toronto a few days after holding up the championship trophy, she was greeted with a welcome befitting a superstar.

Thousands turned up for a rally in her hometown of Mississauga, a Toronto suburb. A street was renamed in her honor. The following Monday was declared "Bianca Andreescu Day" by Toronto mayor John Tory.

Williams was full of praise for Andreescu during the US Open trophy ceremony. (Photo: AP Images)

More than one in every five Canadians watched at least part of her victory on television.

It was the country's most-watched broadcast since the Toronto Raptors clinched the 2019 NBA Championship.

But this isn't basketball, or hockey.

It's tennis, a niche sport in a primarily winter-sport nation that, even if it had been gaining traction in recent years with the success of Milos Raonic and Genie Bouchard on the international stage, remained well off the radar for many of the country's sports fans.

In the U.S., ESPN ratings for the match tied the network's all-time ratings for a US Open telecast.

American fans may have tuned in to see Williams make history; along the way, they discovered a new star.

But as much as many sports fans may have been discovering Andreescu for the very first time, the teenager already had put together a season that defied all expectations—even as she missed more than four months with a shoulder injury through the spring and summer.

It began in Auckland, New Zealand, in January, when Andreescu made a run through the qualifying all the way to the final of the tournament.

But in reality, it began more than a decade ago, when a nine-year-old newly returned to Canada from two years in her parents' native Romania arrived at the Ontario Racquet Club in Mississauga and took her first group lessons.

There were moments of uncertainty. And Andreescu had more than her share of injuries that threatened to derail her dream in those formative years.

But she never gave up. And neither did those who believed in her.

Every elite athlete has a story to tell—a unique journey to the top that has its own mountains to climb and pot holes to leap over.

This is Andreescu's story. ●

Thousands attended a "She the North" rally in Andreescu's hometown after her US Open victory, and a street was renamed in her honour. (Photo: AP Images)

RESERVÉE
UNIQUEMENT
AUX JOUEURS

REST
ONLY P

LES PETITS AS

IT TAKES A VILLAGE TO MAKE A CHAMPION

As Bianca Andreescu took over the spotlight in women's tennis in 2019, she had a revolving support team around her that continued to increase in size and scope; among them were coach Sylvain Bruneau, agent Jonathan Dasnières de Veigy of Octagon, associate coach Isade Juneau, hitting partner Hugo di Feo, strength and conditioning coaches Virginie Tremblay and Clément Golliet, and physiotherapist Kirstin Bauer.

And, back home, she could call upon the services of a sports psychologist and various medical specialists.

But long before that, it took a village to make a champion.

The journey to Andreescu's "overnight success" began when she was six years old with a random introduction to the game on a trip back to Romania to visit her grandparents.

A year later, when she moved back to Romania as her mother started a trucking business, she took to the game in earnest.

"Bianca tried a lot of sports, but she liked tennis the most. She started playing in Pitesti, and her first coach was Gabriel Hristache," mother Maria said in a 2016 interview with ProSports, a Romanian media outlet.

Andreescu, standing between coach Aref Jallali and father Nicu, won Les Petits As in 2014, considered the world championship for players 14 and under. (Photo: Aref Jallali)

Maria Andreescu added that the coach tried to turn her little girl into a left-handed player. But that didn't stick.

When the family returned to the Toronto suburb of Mississauga two years later, Andreescu began group lessons at the nearby Ontario Racquet Club.

"She was a late bloomer. In her first year, she didn't qualify for provincials, even," Tomaz Blazejewski, one of her first coaches, told the *Toronto Star* back in January.

But she picked it up quickly.

When she reached the final of the national outdoor under-12 championships in Mont-Tremblant, Quebec, two years later, things escalated quickly.

Andreescu lost that final to another Toronto-area player of Romanian extraction, Maria Tanasescu.

After the defeat, she and her parents met a Tennis Canada coach named Aref Jallali over coffee at the well-known ski resort.

By then, Tennis Canada was four years into a national development program put in place by Frenchman Louis Borfiga.

Above: Andreescu and coach Aref Jallali, who laid the foundation for her game. (Photo: Aref Jallali) Opposite: Andreescu won the 16-and-under division at the prestigious Orange Bowl in 2014, then reached the 14-and-under final the next week—on a different surface. (Photo: Colette Lewis/Zoo Tennis)

Andreescu had been invited to join a junior regional program established in Toronto in 2009 as a pathway for promising youngsters aspiring to the full national high-performance program established in 2007 in Montreal.

Jallali, the late Bruno Agostinelli, and Lan Yao-Gallop were the coaches. Golliet was the physical trainer.

Jallali, a Tunisian, set out to pour the foundation of the varied, complete game Andreescu possesses today.

He said he met with some resistance from male coaches and executives who wondered why he was teaching a young girl how to hit a slice, or why they practiced her volleys so much when so few in the women's game ever approached the net.

"To develop a player is an art. You need to look, you need to see, you need to add. So I look forward, and I work backward," Jallali said. "You look at what the final picture is, and you slowly add little bits and at the end, you have the picture you had from the start."

As Andreescu got stronger, she began hitting the inside-out and inside-in forehands that are a trademark of men's tennis, but fairly rare on the women's side where most players hit the ball flat and hard.

"For me it was always in my mind, if a girl can open up the court, the rest is easy,"

Jallali said. "We had a very versatile game. And I honestly thought that's the game of the future. You can't go wrong with it."

At the time, there were four promising young Ontarians in the under-14 program: Andreescu, Tanasescu, Anca Craciun, and Brindtha Ramasamy.

Tanasescu, a small girl who hit dinks, slices, and loopy balls and used to drive Andreescu

A year after winning the junior division, 15-year-old Andreescu won the Orange Bowl 18-and-under crown. (Photo: André Labelle/Tennis Canada)

crazy, had the upper hand in their rivalry at that age and was considered by many to be a better prospect.

But it was Andreescu who broke through first.

With Jallali at her side, the 13-year-old Andreescu first appeared on the international tennis radar in 2014 with a win at the prestigious Les Petits As tournament.

That was when she knew she wanted to be a professional tennis player.

"It really gave me a taste of what the Tour felt like. Because after matches, you would sign autographs, you would give interviews, and the stadium court was actually really big and a lot of people came and watched," Andreescu said. "I loved every moment out there. I love playing on big stages and being an inspiration for others."

It was with Jallali that Andreescu began to keep a notebook to record her thoughts, and her tactics against various opponents.

He got the idea from long-time ATP pro Fabrice Santoro, who travelled with two laptop computers full of data from every single match he played.

Tennis Canada coach André Labelle came on board in January 2015 .

Jallali had Andreescu fill the notebook with her goals—not only her goals for that season, but for two or three years down the line.

For every opponent, he had her record her tactics. "It started like that," he said.

Andreescu still uses the notebook today.

The Coaching Village Grows

By the age of 14, Andreescu was under the tutelage of Frenchman Christophe Lambert, who had been hired in late 2013 as head coach of the junior program. With him, she won the prestigious Orange Bowl 16-and-under tournament.

But Lambert left Tennis Canada and returned to Asia, where he coached Chinese player Zhe Li and then became high-performance director for Tennis New Zealand.

Enter Tennis Canada coach André Labelle, and former world No. 3 and 1998 Wimbledon finalist Nathalie Tauziat.

Labelle, who had been working in Florida, first met Andreescu at tri-annual national camps when she was in the regional program.

When he moved to Toronto to replace Lambert as head of the regional center, he and Tauziat were put in charge.

Former world No. 3 Nathalie Tauziat of France (far right) joined Team Bianca in February 2015. (Photo: André Labelle/Tennis Canada)

Tauziat, based in Biarritz, France, mostly travelled with Andreescu to tournaments. Labelle's focus was on the training blocks at home.

Andreescu clearly was ready to be promoted to the national high-performance program in Montreal. But mother Maria would have left her job in Toronto to move there with her. And they likely would have had to hire another coach there, Labelle said.

After parents and federation officials discussed the matter, it was decided that an exception would be made, and the highly promising Andreescu could stay at home while she trained to become a champion.

Already, the family had moved from faraway Mississauga to another suburb, Vaughn, located a mere 15-minute drive north of the national center.

"The parents had confidence in me; they'd known me since the 12-and-unders. So it was decided she would stay home, that this was the best for her," Labelle said. "It was a first (for the program), but it seemed to be the right choice."

Tauziat's philosophy was that Andreescu needed to move up in the court and take the ball earlier.

During that period, there's no doubt that the teenager improved from the baseline. She got more solid in the rallies. But she gave up a little bit of the creativity, the elements of her game that threw her opponents' timing off and that she enjoyed implementing so much.

As a former Wimbledon finalist, coach Nathalie Tauziat was invaluable in helping Andreescu navigate her first Wimbledon as a pro, in 2017.

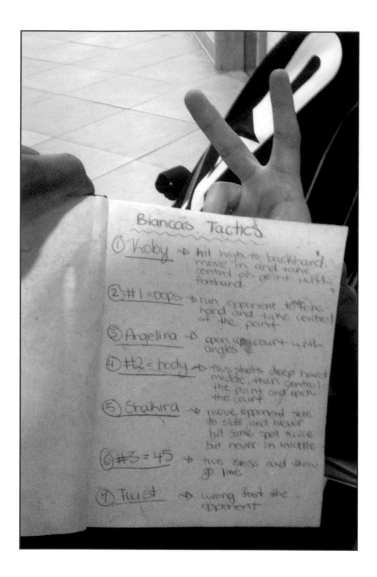

"There was a period where we might have insisted on her hitting the ball early, early, early. But we quickly realized she hit such a heavy ball, it was probably better that she back off the baseline a little bit to take advantage," Labelle said.

In the big picture, it was a slight step back in order to take two steps forward,

a testament to what can happen when a coaching staff takes a long-term view.

Sylvain Bruneau Joins the Team

By then, Sylvain Bruneau had come into the picture.

Bruneau, the head of the Canadian women's tennis program, was also then the Fed Cup captain. Andreescu was progressing to the point where she shortly would become a member of the team, and began to attend training camps Bruneau organized.

Labelle said Bruneau would evoke the game of former champion Kim Clijsters. The Belgian Hall of Famer hit the same heavy ball from the baseline—but she could also come to the net and finish off points.

The next step was to work on Andreescu's fitness and endurance.

"We said to ourselves, she has a good physical profile. But the cardio needs work, and she needs to watch her weight," Labelle said. The services of a nutritionist were added. "It takes some time to put in place. But I think she is at an ideal weight now," he added.

Improved fitness and endurance led to improved decision-making and shot selection.

Above: Andreescu began filling a notebook with thoughts and tactics before she hit her teens. Opposite: Five years later, as a pro, she was still doing it. (Photos: André Labelle/Tennis Canada, Aref Jallali)

"With all the tactical choices she had, she was able to do a little bit of everything. It takes a certain amount of time to learn to make the right choices, choose the right combination of shots. But you have to be able to stay in the point, as well," Labelle said. "Back then, when the point was a little too long, she rushed to finish it. So she would make poor shot choices. But being in shape, knowing you won't finish the match on one leg, she improved on all those aspects."

Labelle said the confidence in her fitness made Andreescu more intelligent on court. "She understands better how she's going to win her points, and what to do specifically against certain opponents," he said. "And the great thing with her is that you can make up any match plan, and she can execute it."

By early 2018, Tauziat's mandate was up. And Tennis Canada decided Bruneau would step down as Fed Cup captain and coach Andreescu full time.

When they headed to Japan that winter to start somewhat from scratch after a challenging 2017, he took her to watch some of the men play.

And the foundation that had been put in place by the forward-thinking Jallali early on was taken to a new level.

"She was already 250 in the world and she was 17. I felt she could do more on the court. I felt she could do more than just hit the ball really early and hard and through the court, which she was doing. So we looked at a lot of the guys, what they were doing, the way they were playing tennis I think with more shape and with more spin and using the entire court," Bruneau said.

"I'm a big, big fan of her game. I think she's got wonderful hands. She understands tennis. She sees the court. She understands the importance of (hitting) different shots and not always the same shot over and over and over again," he added.

At this point in a seven-year journey, Bruneau believes Andreescu has the full package.

"If we look from an athletic standpoint, she's a great athlete. She's strong. She's fast. We see the way she covers the court. And then you look at her mental aspect. She's as tough as it gets as a competitor. She's not scared. She goes for it. The bigger the occasion, the bigger she hits," he said.

"So when you put all of that together—the athletic, the mental, and her game style, which is a little different, obviously—you've got Bianca." ●

Behind every successful player is a team to take care of both body and mind. Sylvain Bruneau (right) is the head coach of Team Bianca.

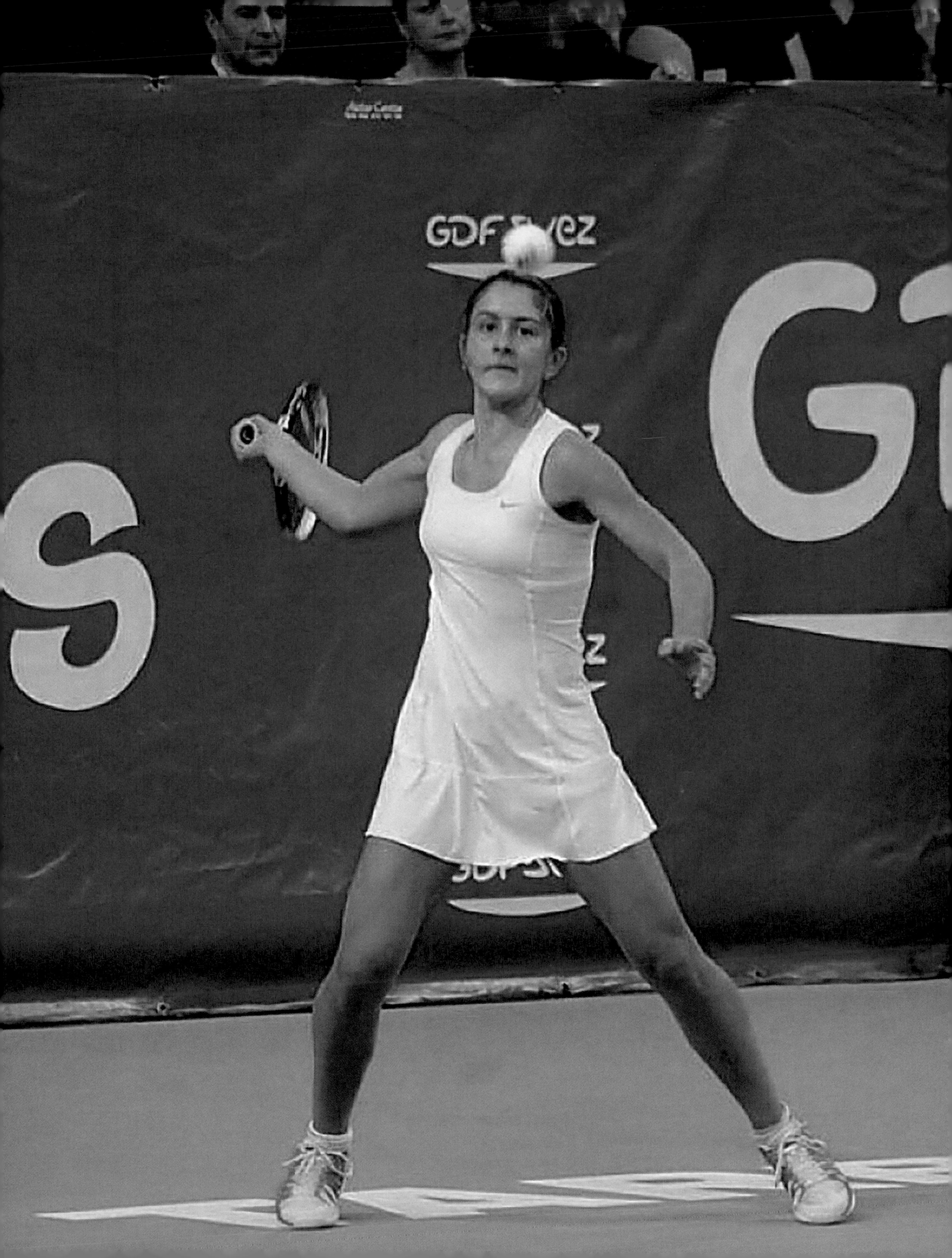

2

SETTING THE STAGE

Bianca Andreescu's early days were spent at the Ontario Racquet Club, a private club near her home in Mississauga.

She was progressing well.

The 11-year-old had just lost in the final of the under-12 outdoor national championships in Mont-Tremblant, Quebec, when she and her parents first met Tennis Canada coach Aref Jallali.

From that point, he became her main coach as she was accepted into the under-14 national program at Toronto's Rexall Centre (home of the Rogers Cup) along with three other talented young Ontarians: Anca Craciun, Brindtha Ramasamy (who won that under-12 final), and Maria Tanasescu (with whom Andreescu won the under-12 doubles title).

Randomly, three of the four were of Romanian descent.

Jallali and the Tennis Canada team laid down the foundations of the all-court game that was on such brilliant display during Andreescu's 2019 season.

Under-14 Supremacy at Les Petit As

The city of Tarbes, France, population 40,000 and just 60 miles from the Spanish border, comes alive in January when it hosts the most unlikely of "big events."

Les Petits As (The Little Aces) is the unofficial world championship for 14-and-under players.

At 13, Andreescu announced her arrival by winning the Les Petit As, considered the world championship for players 14 and under. (Photo: Aref Jallali)

It draws big crowds. And virtually every big name you see at the top level today has played it.

Among the former Petits As champions are Rafael Nadal (2000), American Frances Tiafoe (2012), 2017 French Open champion Jelena Ostapenko (2011), former No. 1 Kim Clijsters (1997), and Martina Hingis (1991–92)

In 2014, at age 13 after two years in the Tennis Canada program, Andreescu joined that illustrious group.

It's not always indicative of future success. For example, Ukraine's Dayana Yastremska, the only teenager other than Andreescu near the top 25 as 2019 draws to a close, lost in the first round that year.

But a victory such as this one puts a player officially on the radar.

And Andreescu raised even more eyebrows when, still just 14, she capped off her 2014 season by winning the 16-and-under title at the prestigious Orange Bowl in Florida.

She was the fourth consecutive Canadian girl to win that title although, so far, the only one to have made her mark in the pros.

2015 Canadian Junior of the Year

Andreescu began playing the International Tennis Federation junior circuit, where the tournaments are rated from Grade 5 (the lowest) up to Grade 1, with the biggest events of all rated "Grade A."

In her third ITF event, Andreescu won the singles at a Grade 5 tournament in Havana, Cuba.

She won a Grade 4 event in South Carolina that November. And in February 2015, on a three-tournament tour of South American with fellow Canadian Isabelle Boulais, she won the singles and doubles at a Grade 2 tournament in Bolivia.

By now, former world No. 3 and 1998 Wimbledon finalist Nathalie Tauziat, a Frenchwoman, who worked for Tennis Canada as a coach and helped Andreescu's fellow Canadian Eugenie Bouchard win the 2012 Wimbledon junior doubles title, was on board. So was longtime Tennis Canada coach André Labelle.

But then, they had to miss the second tournament, in Chile.

"There weren't many direct flights. And they couldn't get there in time for the first round. And they wouldn't wait for her," Labelle recalled. "We wrote a letter, contacted the ITF. They couldn't do anything."

After an unexpected week off, Andreescu did get to the third tournament, in Buenos Aires, and reached the final.

Andreescu was the fourth consecutive Canadian girl to win the Orange Bowl 16s—but the first to break through in a big way as a professional. (Photo: Colette Lewis/Zoo Tennis)

Andreescu made her junior Grand Slam debut at age 14, at the French Open in Paris.

After those results, and more victories in a series of top-level junior events in France in the spring, Andreescu—still 14—had a junior ranking high enough to get her into qualifying for her first junior Grand Slam, the 2015 French Open.

"When you perform well in those Grade 2 events, you move up quickly," Labelle said. "That's how she got started."

Paris was a first taste of the big time on one of the tennis world's grandest stages, as the teenager won two qualifying matches and faced Russian Anna Kalinskaya in the first round of the main draw.

Already, Andreescu's full arsenal was on display. If you walked by the court that day, you saw a 14-year-old hit slices and drop shots, look for any opportunity to approach the net, and hit hard from the baseline. She was an attention-getter.

And she certainly caught Kalinskaya's attention when she won the first set 6-0.

But then the rains came. And Kalinskaya, far more experienced at that level, handled the delays and the challenging conditions deftly in an 0-6, 6-3, 6-2 victory.

Still, Andreescu was on her way.

Andreescu played junior Wimbledon as well. She lost in the first round to American

Sofia Kenin—a rival she would later meet on several occasions in her breakout 2019 professional season.

"Since the French Open I had problems with my ankle and my thigh, but I just took weeks off and got my head straight," Andreescu said later when reflecting on the 2015 season. "After that I think I played my best tennis so far."

Andreescu, along with teammates Charlotte Robillard-Millette and Vanessa Wong, won bronze at the 2015 Junior Fed Cup final for players aged 16-and-under. Andreescu won all five of her singles matches, and four of her five doubles matches.

She then returned to the Orange Bowl and won the biggest title, as a 15-year-old in the 18-and-under division.

"It was like on and off. I tried to really not focus on the win and everything, and the rain, just focus on my game and just play my best," Andreescu told ITF journalist Sandra Harwitt. "I'm only 15, and this is like the next step to winning a Grand Slam."

Andreescu finished inside the top 10 in the ITF junior girls' rankings. And she was named Tennis Canada's junior girls' player of the year for 2015.

Rain delays in Paris were too much for the rookie to handle, but she used that experience to her advantage in the Orange Bowl final.

Stress (Fractures) in Australia

After a 2015 junior season during which she spent a significant time on the red clay, Andreescu traveled Down Under to start the 2016 season on hard courts.

She had big goals.

"I want to try to do even better than I did in 2015. I would like to win a junior Grand Slam, and to reach No. 1 in the rankings, and be top 250 on the WTA Tour," she said, with all the insouciance of youth.

Australia was on the other side of the world, farther than the 15-year-old had ever traveled in her life. And it wasn't an easy trip.

There was a 10-hour layover in Los Angeles. And Andreescu had a middle seat for the 16-hour flight from L.A. to Melbourne, Australia.

"I slept most of the way. But the person in the window seat kept wanting to get up, so I got up and walked a bit and stretched," she said. "I wore compression socks. They really help."

Andreescu was all braces and smiles. And she was the favorite.

"There's a bit of pressure being the No. 1 seed but I try not to let that affect me. I just play tennis," she said before the Australian Open juniors got under way.

Andreescu's 2016 junior debut at the Australian Open was cut short by injuries that would keep her off the court for six months.

The previous week, Andreescu had been forced to withdraw before her quarterfinal match at Traralgon, a tune-up for the main event.

"It was an abductor strain, so I got that checked out. After a week, it got better, but it came back a month later. So I took another week off. And then it stopped, and it came back last week in Traralgon and I had to retire," she said. "But now it's looking perfect so hopefully I can get through the whole tournament."

She couldn't. Andreescu reached the third round of both the singles and doubles. But then, she had to withdraw.

Beyond the abductor—a recurring theme—she had a stress fracture in her foot.

Andreescu wouldn't return to the court until July.

"That was a bit of a black period. But you do the best you can," coach André Labelle said.

Playing Tennis in a Chair

Andreescu was still on court every day—an hour a day, sitting on a five-wheeled chair. They worked her groundstrokes, her slice, her drop shots, and her serve.

"She always had issues with her (service) toss. And I used to joke with her that her toss was better in the chair," Labelle said.

There were two stress fractures. And Labelle said they were similar to the types ballerinas suffer from, and in very awkward, delicate places to treat. So it was going to take time.

"We were expecting five or six weeks, but it was more like three months. Still, she was getting better," he said. "She couldn't put weight on her legs. But she improved her skills. And we worked on the physical side."

Andreescu would head to the center in Toronto, get treatment, and go to the pool. "She has a good mentality," Labelle said. "She doesn't get discouraged. She stays positive. And I think the parents did a good job, too. They kept her busy."

Left: Andreescu teamed with Charlotte Robillard-Millette in doubles at the 2016 junior Australian Open. Opposite: Andreescu reached the semifinal at the 2016 junior US Open.

Andreescu returned just before junior Wimbledon in July. She bowed out in the third round.

She then reached the US Open junior singles semifinal, losing to longtime junior rival Kayla Day of the U.S.

After wrapping up the season on the professional circuit in October, Andreescu would return in January for her final—and best—junior campaign.

Hardware in Melbourne

As the No. 7 seed, Andreescu wasn't a favourite at the 2017 junior Australian Open. But junior rankings can be somewhat deceiving; many of the better older players are already making the transition to the professional ranks, and don't play a lot of junior events that can bump up their rankings.

Elena Rybakina of Russia was the No. 16 seed in that girls' singles draw. Rybakina (now representing Kazakhstan) reached the top 50 on the WTA Tour in the fall of 2019.

American Caty McNally, then just 15 years old and seeded No. 12, took a set off Serena Williams at this year's US Open and already has won a WTA Tour doubles title.

And Iga Swiatek, also 15 at the time, was the No. 8 seed. She reached the round of 16 in the women's singles at the French Open in 2019, and broke into the top 50 in the rankings in August.

So it was a quality field. And Andreescu reached the semifinal without dropping a set and with her left leg encased in an almost cast-like wrap from the top of the leg right down to the knee.

In the semifinal she met Rebeka Masarova, a powerhouse Swiss player a year her senior who won the junior French Open title the previous spring.

Andreescu nearly had it, on a very hot day. But despite coming inches from winning the match in straight sets, she fell to Masarova 4-6, 7-6 (5), 6-0.

If there was disappointment, the Canadian didn't let it affect her as she set out to win the doubles with Carson Branstine, an American-turned-Canadian from Southern California who had become a good friend.

The duo brought home the doubles trophy, beating Swiatek and countrywoman Maja Chwalinska in the final.

Doubles contribute a share in the calculation of the ITF junior rankings. So at the end of that Australian Open, Andreescu reached her career-best of No. 3.

Andreescu and Carson Branstine captured the 2017 Australian Open junior girls' doubles title.

A Junior Finale in Paris

As she turned 17, her focus now squarely on making the transition to the professional ranks, Andreescu played one final junior tournament.

It was at the French Open, where she had played her first junior Grand Slam just...two years before?

Somehow, as eventful as it had been, it felt so much longer ago than that.

As it turned out, the Les Petits As tournament back in 2014 was the beginning of a junior career arc that ended back in France, three and a half years later.

Andreescu defeated former No. 1 junior Claire Liu in the Petits As final. And Liu ended Andreescu's junior singles career by defeating her in the quarterfinal in Paris.

Andreescu had reached the Les Petits As doubles final as well, with Tanasescu. They lost to Russians Oleysa Pervushina and Anastasia Potapova.

In the 2017 French Open junior girls' doubles final, Andreescu and Branstine beat that same Russian pair to win the title and wrap up Andreescu's junior career.

It was a perfect ending, a full circle.

From now on, Andreescu would put all of her focus on climbing the WTA Tour rankings. ●

As Andreescu closed out her junior career at the 2017 French Open, she also played in the qualifying of the pro event.

3

ENTERING THE PRO RANKS

Bianca Andreescu had barely begun her junior career in earnest when she also began taking her first baby steps in the pro ranks.

At 15, she made her professional debut at a small International Tennis Federation tournament in Gatineau, Quebec, across the river from the Canadian capital in Ottawa.

She reached the final.

The next week, she made her first appearance at her big hometown tournament.

The Rogers Cup, which has the ATP and WTA Tour playing the same week and alternating between Montreal and Toronto, was in Toronto that year.

The debut wasn't an auspicious one. Instead of facing entry-level competition as she had in Gatineau, she ran up against an experienced player from Belarus, Olga Govortsova.

After a competitive first set, she fell 7-5, 6-0.

Andreescu played one more pro tournament in Toronto that fall, again losing in the first round.

Andreescu wasn't winning many matches at that level. But she was gaining valuable experience. And that's the point of the exercise at that stage.

But after that, she focused on the junior circuit until the following summer.

When she returned to Gatineau a year later, now 16, she not only defended her singles title, she won the doubles as well.

Andreescu made her hometown Rogers Cup debut in 2015, at age 15. Four years later, she won the title.

Her efforts raised her WTA Tour ranking close to the top 400—a full 200 spots higher than she had been at the start of the 2016 season.

That October, she reached the finals in both singles and doubles at a much bigger tournament, a $50,000 ITF event in Saguenay, Quebec.

By the end of the season, Andreescu had broken into the top 300 in the rankings.

Those leaps in the rankings are relatively easier at that stage. One good week can mean 100 spots.

And, at that stage, it's almost easier for the top juniors to play the professional ranks. When they compete in junior tournaments as favorites, they are the hunted. When they show up at a pro event that includes many women in their 20s who are still trying to climb the ranks, and for whom every match win might mean the difference between continuing to chase their dream and facing reality, they are the hunter. Relatively speaking, that's the easier role.

Which doesn't make it any less challenging.

Andreescu won her second career pro title in Rancho Santa Fe, California, in February 2017, beating American Kayla Day in the $25,000 final. (Photo: André Labelle/Tennis Canada)

2017: A Year of Firsts, and of Struggles

After playing the Australian junior circuit to start the 2017 season, Andreescu began putting together winning streaks at the $25,000 level in the pros. She went 15-2 through the end of April, and jumped into the top 200.

She had earned the right to compete at her first Grand Slam in the senior ranks, at the French Open in the qualifying. She lost in the first round.

"Before that, I hadn't played a match in a month. So I think I was kind of all over the place," Andreescu said.

Andreescu played the junior event in Paris the following week. And she capped off her junior career by winning a second junior Grand Slam doubles title, again with Carson Branstine.

The tennis gods—and her injuries—had somewhat conspired against her. So it wasn't in the cards for her to win the big singles title that is the cherry on the cake of any player's

Above: Parents Maria and Nicu were on hand in 2017 when Andreescu qualified for her first Grand Slam main draw at Wimbledon. Opposite: Reaching both the singles and doubles final of a $50,000 tournament in Saguenay, Quebec, in October 2016 was Andreescu's best early pro result. She lost to American CiCi Bellis (left). (Photo: André Labelle/Tennis Canada)

junior career, as her fellow Canadians Genie Bouchard and Filip Peliwo had done back in 2012.

But now, just as she was celebrating her 17th birthday, it was time to leave that behind and become a full-time pro.

And it all began at Wimbledon.

First Grand Slam Main Draw

With her parents on hand, Andreescu strolled through the women's singles qualifying event at Roehampton.

She didn't drop a set in three match wins that put her into the main draw, and earned her the right to proudly walk through the doors of the legendary All-England Lawn Tennis and Croquet Club as a full-fledged professional competitor.

The day that a player can trade in their "qualifier's" accreditation for the real thing at Wimbledon is a landmark day.

"With (former coach) Nathalie (Tauziat), I discussed that on grass you have to be aggressive. So in my mind, I just told myself to go for it. And I made it. I played a couple of tournaments before this so I got kind of used to the grass," Andreescu said. "Qualifying for a Grand Slam is just incredible, I'm so happy. But I have one day to celebrate a bit. And then it's back to work."

After winning three qualifying matches, Andreescu made her Grand Slam debut at Wimbledon in 2017.

In her WTA Tour debut, Andreescu reached the quarterfinal.

The historic All-England Club is, at most, a 15-minute drive from the Bank of England Sports Ground where the qualifying takes place.

But it's a world away.

The qualifying site is essentially a big field where they put up fences and nets and paint lines for a few weeks. The AELTC is a perfect gem—a genteel, manicured piece of tennis perfection that looks even more surreal in real life than it does on television.

Andreescu lost in the first round of the main draw to Kristina Kucova of Slovakia.

But her breakthrough wasn't far away.

First Big Win in D.C.

As her WTA Tour ranking approached No. 150, Andreescu was given a wild card into the Citi Open, a lower-level WTA Tour event in Washington, D.C.

It's a joint event, where the men's tournament is a much higher "ATP 500" competition. So the women can get somewhat lost in the shuffle.

But Andreescu quickly made her mark in her WTA Tour main draw debut.

She had recently turned professional, choosing the Octagon agency to represent her interests.

They weren't overly awed by her prospects at that point. A representative from the company came up to her one day on the site, introduced himself, and told her he was available should she need anything.

And that was pretty much that.

But Andreescu made it impossible not to pay attention.

She opened the tournament with a hard-fought, three-set win over Camila Giorgi, a hard-hitting Italian player whose power, when on, makes it difficult to create anything on the court.

This was especially true as the court they played on was by far the fastest of all the match courts.

"It was coming so fast. I was hitting all my forehands like Nadal, I swear," Andreescu

Andreescu's debut at the Citi Open in Washington, D.C., in August 2017 brought her first win over a top-20 player.

Andreescu practices with countrywoman Françoise Abanda before her first-round match at Wimbledon in 2017.

said, mimicking the Spaniard's stroke finish up behind his head. "It just skidded."

She followed that up with a 6-2, 6-3 upset win over the No. 2 seed, France's Kristina Mladenovic, who was ranked No. 13 in the world.

(That loss would be the first of a 14-match streak of futility for the Frenchwoman, a streak that would only be broken six months later in St. Petersburg, Russia.)

German veteran Andrea Petkovic was too much for Andreescu in the quarterfinal.

"I'd never seen her play the way she played that first set against Petkovic," André

Labelle said. "But she wasn't able to keep the intensity."

But as debuts go, it was impressive.

"I tried. Trust me, I tried. She just played really well in the end," Andreescu said of the Petkovic match. "Beating a top-20 player (in Mladenovic) is what I've worked for my entire career. So I'm very proud of myself. I sure gained a lot of experience and confidence playing here."

Andreescu's biggest struggle that week was the fact that the laundry service had turned her match outfits into a set of six incredibly shrinking red Nike mini-dresses.

Luckily the outfits came with longer stretch shorts, or her debut might have become a memorable one for all the wrong reasons!

Rogers Cup Main Draw Debut

The rest of the 2017 season didn't go nearly as well.

Andreescu finally made her Rogers Cup main draw debut in Toronto on a wild card, but was beaten by Hungary's Timea Babos.

Through November, she won only one singles match during a stretch that included a trip to Europe to play WTA Tour events in Luxembourg and Linz, Austria.

With Coach Tauziat's mandate up, Tennis Canada was trying out another coach in view of the 2018 season. But it wasn't a particularly good fit.

From a high ranking of No. 143 after Washington, Andreescu ended the season at No. 189.

Those growing pains are to be expected with fledgling pros as they transition from the smaller tournaments to the big time.

In the big picture, still just 17, the future remained bright.

Part of the development process as a pro is to increase the off-court training in the gym, to get stronger and more resistant to injuries.

A Holding Pattern in 2018— and Back Woes

After making the trip to Australia—this time as a pro—Andreescu won just two games in a first-round qualifying loss to Alexandra Dulgheru of Romania.

It was a setback defeat.

And after one more tournament back in North America, Andreescu headed off to Japan to get back to basics at a series of $25,000 events.

Coach André Labelle was there for the first tournament in Toyota, and drove her to the next stop in Kofu.

Sylvain Bruneau, Fed Cup captain and head of women's tennis in Canada, was there with another player, Rebecca Marino.

It was the beginning of the coaching relationship with Andreescu, and they looked for a spark.

"With Sylvain, we reworked her game, so that it was much more like the game she plays now," Labelle said.

Andreescu reached finals in Kofu and Kashiwa, and seemed to be back on track.

One Tough Summer

After a month's training break at home, Andreescu arrived in Paris to try to qualify for her first French Open main draw.

She almost made it.

After breezing through her first two rounds, she succumbed to Richel Hogenkamp of the Netherlands on a gloomy, drizzly afternoon. Andreescu had opportunities to take it to a third set but she couldn't convert them.

Andreescu also fell in the final round of qualifying at Wimbledon. And through the summer, her back woes intensified.

She had to withdraw before a quarterfinal match at a $60,000 tournament in Granby, Quebec, even though she had managed, with some on-court treatment, to get through the first few rounds.

But Andreescu had to skip the Rogers Cup that year. And even when she arrived in New York at the end of August to try her luck in the US Open qualifying, she was a long way from healthy.

The Canadian managed to complete her first-round match against Serbian teenager Olga Danilovic. But it was clear she was hampered, and she lost in straight sets.

She wouldn't return to the court for another two months.

In retrospect, Andreescu has said that the break was a good thing.

In 2018, back woes dogged Andreescu the entire summer, including here at the Granby Challenger in Quebec.

She needed to get healthy. And there was a lot going on off the court that she needed to sort through.

"I wasn't going through a good period in my life at that point. I was having problems with some relationships in my life, with my body, and even my mind, too," Andreescu said.

When she returned on the minor-league circuit in the fall, she finished off the season with an 18–3 run in singles, and two titles.

If ending the tennis season in November meant that her off-season would be cut short,

the boost of confidence and belief that she was back on the right path was a good trade-off.

After dropping below No. 240 in the world while she was out—likely too low to play the Australian Open qualifying in January 2019—she raised that number to No. 152 by season's end.

She couldn't know then that 2019 would be beyond even her loftiest expectations, and that that "No. 152" would rapidly disappear in the rear-view mirror. ●

Opposite: Right from the start of 2018, Andreescu's season was compromised by injuries. Above: Back woes played a large role in Andreescu's first-round qualifying loss at the 2018 US Open. A year later, she returned and won the title.

AUCKLAND, INDIAN WELLS, AND BEYOND

If Bianca Andreescu's first full season in the professional ranks was a learning experience, the 18-year-old was determined to do everything possible to make sure she took a step up in 2019.

Among her goals was to be ranked high enough by the spring to gain direct entry into the French Open.

A preseason training camp at the famed IMG Academy in Bradenton, Florida, was just the ticket.

It's not unusual to see Canadians in Florida in the winter; the snowbirds dot the state from October to April. And that's also true at the academy.

There, she could reconnect with fellow up-and-coming Canadian teenagers Félix Auger-Aliassime and Denis Shapovalov, with whom she had spent much of her time in the juniors. A group of Tennis Canada coaches and support stuff also migrated down south for December.

Andreescu later said that her preseason was everything she could have asked for.

And as the new year approached, she headed to New Zealand to begin the season.

Andreescu reached the singles final in Auckland, falling to Germany's Julia Goerges. (Photo: AP Images)

With a ranking outside the top 150, scheduling during what's called the "Australian summer" can be a little tricky.

There are typically two weeks of warmup tournaments before the Australian Open. And with Andreescu's ranking, the second week must be used to try to get through the qualifying tournament.

So she only had one week to acclimate and prepare.

The previous year, ranked just inside the top 200, Andreescu opted to start at a $25,000 ITF tournament in Playford, just north of Adelaide, Australia.

This year, she was the No. 5 seed in qualifying at the smaller of the two WTA tournaments that week, in Auckland, New Zealand.

Andreescu rolled through her first two matches before outlasting the feisty German, Laura Siegemund, in the final round to earn a spot in the main draw.

Coach Sylvain Bruneau was not on hand. He had returned to Canada after the preseason to spend a few days during the holidays with his young family, and was to meet Andreescu in Melbourne the following week.

Andreescu and strength and conditioning coach Virginie Tremblay were a force as Andreescu went from the qualifying to the final in Auckland to start the season. (Photo: AP Images)

Andreescu prepares for the Australian Open under the watchful eye of Tremblay and coach Sylvain Bruneau.

So it was a "girls' trip": just Andreescu and Tennis Canada's Virginie Tremblay—a young, vibrant woman who is a skilled kinesiologist and strength and conditioning coach, and whose positive energy is contagious.

Tremblay also played tennis as a junior, a part of her résumé that would come in handy.

The beginning of the tennis season—just like the end of the season—is prime time for upsets. Few of the top players are match tough as they hit their first competitive balls of the season. There's significant jet lag to overcome, and it's a great opportunity for upstarts to make a move.

And that's exactly what Andreescu did.

With on-court coaching available on the WTA Tour, it was Tremblay who occasionally went out to offer reassurance and perhaps a few words of advice.

She became a mini-star of her own as the cameras regularly panned to her—much to her embarrassment.

The all-girl combination proved tough to beat.

From the hard-hitting Timea Babos to reigning Australian Open champion Caroline Wozniacki to the legendary Venus Williams,

Andreescu blazed her way through to the final.

In her eighth match of the week, against the defending champion Julia Georges, Andreescu was just a few points away from winning her first WTA Tour title. Ultimately, she ran out of fuel against the veteran German and succumbed 2-6, 7-5, 6-1.

"I can't really describe it. It was a dream come true, and I'm just beyond grateful," she said of her dream run upon arrival in Melbourne a few days later. "I was just going for my shots. I know I didn't have anything to lose, and I did just that. And it seemed like it worked."

Andreescu's ranking leaped from No. 152 to No. 107.

It was too late to be considered for entry into the Australian Open main draw, for which the deadline was six weeks prior to the event.

But the Tuesday start for the qualifying rounds meant that the updated rankings from the Monday could be factored in. And so, Andreescu ended up with the No. 4 seed and a more favorable draw.

The way she was playing, it might not have much mattered anyway. But fate decreed that Andreescu had an easy run anyway.

She had a day off on the Monday, a light practice Tuesday. And by Wednesday, she was ready to go.

Andreescu's first opponent, Katie Swan, was having back issues and was in serious distress in their first-round match. After a quick first set, Swan sat down, her back in spasms with tears rolling down her face, and was forced to retire.

Swan was rolled off the court in a wheelchair.

After a routine 6-4, 6-1 victory over second-round opponent Valentini Grammatikopoulou of Greece, Andreescu benefited again as Tereza Smitkova of the Czech Republic retired down 6-0, 4-1 in the final round.

There was a certain irony to Andreescu's successful run to her first Australian main draw. The teenager who had suffered through back problems in 2018 was the beneficiary of the struggles of two opponents who were dealing with the same issue.

But sometimes being lucky can be as beneficial as being good. And Andreescu barely had to break a sweat—a welcome interlude after all the tennis she had played the previous week.

"I tried to just use last week as good momentum and good confidence. I know that

Andreescu wrapped up her first Australian swing as a professional with an 11-2 record.

Despite a sore back, and extreme heat, Andreescu left Australia ranked in the top 100.

now my name is on the map. I don't want to put any pressure on myself because I know people are going to expect more from me," she said. "Last week I was feeling pretty tired. I played eight matches in nine days—never, ever did that before. I got a lot of treatment done, and it seemed like it worked."

First Main Draw Down Under

The 16 qualifiers are placed randomly, with open spots left on the draw sheet as the singles draw was made on the Thursday.

There were some top-flight players awaiting qualifiers in the first round. Among them were former Australian Open champion Maria Sharapova, and top-ranked players like Elina Svitolina, Karolina Pliskova, and Aryna Sabalenka.

Andreescu avoided them all. She drew Whitney Osuigwe, a 16-year-old American ranked No. 199 who had earned the U.S. Tennis Association's wild card into the tournament.

But it was a tricky matchup nonetheless.

From being the underdog with nothing to lose in Auckland, Andreescu had to pivot into a situation in which she was very much the favourite.

It was a steamy hot day—not unusual during the Australian Open. Several of the male players, who must play best-of-five sets,

were forced to retire. And Andreescu's match against Osuigwe, who was dressed in similar Nike clothing, was a marathon.

Andreescu suffered with cramps in her calves. Her back acted up on her, and she needed treatment on court. The 7-6 (7), 6-7 (0), 6-3 victory took two hours, 45 minutes.

"All I can say is that it's one of the toughest matches I've ever played and I'm so, so, so happy I pulled through," Andreescu said afterward. "I have no idea how I won today. My body was a mess—especially after the first set. I just fought."

The Canadian went on to lose to the experienced Anastasija Sevastova in the second round.

But she had already accomplished two goals: she posted her first victory in the main draw of a Grand Slam tournament, and she broke into the top 100 in the rankings for the first time in her career.

Fruitful Stopover in Newport Beach

On the way back to Canada from Australia, Andreescu stopped in Newport Beach, California, to play a smaller WTA tournament.

It was not a full WTA event, more the equivalent of a top minor-league Challenger tournament.

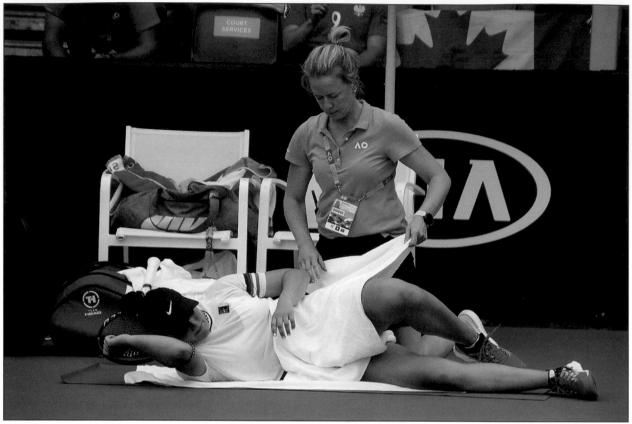

The difference with Andreescu in 2019 was that she overcame her physical challenges, rather than let them overcome her.

Seeded No. 6, the momentum she brought with her helped Andreescu get past four other seeded players to win the biggest title of her career so far.

Among them was Genie Bouchard. Andreescu pummelled her countrywoman 6-2, 6-0 in the quarterfinal.

Even more impressively, she came back from losing the first set in both the semifinal against No. 2 seed Tatjana Maria, and the final against No. 7 seed Jessica Pegula.

Against Pegula, she lost the first set 6-0 before coming back to take the trophy.

Andreescu had won six of her seven three-set matches so far in 2019. And in four of them, she had to come back from a set down.

Between her effort in Australia and the title in Newport Beach, Andreescu's ranking now was up to a career-high No. 68.

Heat and Humidity in Acapulco

After a trip to s'-Hertogenbosch, Netherlands, where she led the Canadian Fed Cup team to a 4-0 sweep of the Dutch side, Andreescu headed to Mexico at the end of February to play a small event in Acapulco.

She was one of the last players to squeeze into the main draw. But she reached the semifinal, losing to American Sofia Kenin 7-5 in the third set.

The good news what that the BNP Paribas Open, a major tournament just below the Grand Slams in importance, had offered her a wild card.

On the basis of her current ranking, she would have earned her way in. But the six-week advance deadline worked against her.

The same week a year ago, Andreescu was losing in the second round of a $25,000 ITF event in Japan to No. 276-ranked Dejana Radanovic of Serbia.

This year, she was in tennis paradise.

From a Wild Card to the Winner's Circle

At this point, Andreescu had played more tennis than anyone on the WTA Tour.

Including the Newport Beach tournament and Fed Cup, she arrived in the idyllic retirement community of Indian Wells, California, with a 21–3 won-loss record.

But it almost went sour right from the first round, when she faced the experienced Romanian Irina-Camelia Begu.

Down a set, spraying errors as she struggled to adjust to the change in

Andreescu was almost out of Indian Wells in the first round, against Irina-Camelia Begu.

conditions from hot, humid Acapulco to the unique combination of thin desert air and a slow, gritty court, Andreescu's defense pulled her through in nearly two and a half hours. Her back was acting up again, as well.

It was yet another three-set comeback to add to her résumé.

"I honestly don't know how I won, because I wasn't feeling so well, and Begu was playing incredible," she said.

Andreescu took that get-out-of-jail-free card and ran through former top-10 player Dominika Cibulkova in the second round, qualifier Stefanie Voegele in the third round, and No. 18 seed Qiang Wang in the round of 16.

"I have watched her play many times on TV, so it's just crazy to think that I'll be competing against her," Andreescu said of her quarterfinal opponent, two-time Grand Slam champion Garbiñe Muguruza.

She thrashed the Spaniard, losing only one game.

"I like to dream big. I think I did make a bit of history the last couple months, but I'm not gonna stop. I'm going to keep going," she said. "And who knows? Maybe if I win this tournament, I'll make even more history."

Andreescu wasn't being completely serious about hoisting the 40-pound trophy.

Or was she?

She was taking it one match at a time—as the old cliché goes—generally unaware of who her next opponent would be even after she had won the previous match. But her mantra had always been this: dream big, and anything is possible.

The Cinderella story was being written. And as is usually the case at Indian Wells, a popular winter destination spot for Canadians from the western part of the country, Andreescu could feed off significant fan support in the stands.

As she attended press conference after press conference, everyone wanted to know everything about her.

Why did she wear that coiled hair tie around her right arm?

For good luck.

What was she sniffing out of a pot on some of the changeovers?

Top secret.

How did she feel about the new wave of Canadian teens including Shapovalov and Auger-Aliassime?

"We're all killing it. It's great."

Everything was new, and everything was somewhat surreal.

Andreescu's go-to phrase had become this: "If someone told me at the beginning

As Andreescu made her way through the Indian Wells draw, she began attracting more and more attention.

A relieved Andreescu moves on to the Indian Wells quarterfinal with another win over a top-20 player, Qiang Wang of China.

of the year that I would *(insert latest accomplishment here)*, I would have told them that they're crazy."

She had to repeat the phrase often. Which didn't make it any less true.

From No. 152 at the start of the season, Andreescu was already going to leap into the top 50 at the end of the BNP Paribas Open.

And she wasn't done.

Shaking and Speechless

Elina Svitolina of Ukraine and Angelique Kerber of Germany did not get to the top of the women's game because of their big serves or incredible power.

They thrived because of a willingness to run, chase, and defend—and pull the trigger on offense when the opportunities presented themselves.

They fed off their opponents' pace. And Kerber had taken that game to the No. 1 ranking and three Grand Slam titles.

In the aftermath of the 6-3, 2-6, 6-4 victory over Svitolina, Andreescu let her emotions flow for the first time.

"I'm actually shaking right now. It's just so incredible. I'm honestly speechless— speechless," she said.

Meanwhile, Andreescu's parents—and Coco the dog—were flying from Toronto to Miami during the match against Svitolina.

They were able to watch it on the plane; there was no way to anticipate the run she was going to make in the California desert.

So the family planned to reunite in Florida.

But first Andreescu had a final to win.

The 6-4, 3-6, 6-4 victory over Kerber in the final featured an inspiring on-court visit from coach Sylvain Bruneau in the third set. He knew just what to say.

Andreescu was physically exhausted. "I can barely move out there," she wailed to Bruneau.

"It becomes a little bit mind over body. You know how strong you are, mentally and physically," he replied. "It's true, you're going to need to push through it. You're going to need to stay strong under adversity. But that's okay. That's what you want—you welcome competition."

"I want this so bad." Andreescu answered.

"That's good. Perfect. So go out there and keep competing every single ball. Every single point."

In such dramatic circumstances, perhaps that little nudge was just enough to make the difference.

"That moment was everything to me. He really helped me in that moment with such

A pep talk from coach Sylvain Bruneau made all the difference in the Indian Wells final. (Photo: AP Images)

incredible words. The way he says things really—it really gives me chills. So I'm glad I called him at that moment," Andreescu said.

Andreescu became the first wild card to win at Indian Wells—and the youngest, at 18, to win it since Serena Williams beat Steffi Graf in the final 20 years earlier.

"I was actually really dizzy in the locker room because there were just so many thoughts and emotions going through my body," Andreescu said.

In an instant, Andreescu was ranked No. 24 in the world. And she was an instant millionaire, thanks to the winner's check for $1,354,010.

But there were warning signs. Andreescu's shoulder had been taped for the final. She said it was "more for prevention," but admitted it had been "really, really tight."

Nevertheless, she headed across the U.S. to another top-level tournament, the Miami Open.

One Tournament Too Many?

In her position, many players might well have pulled out of the Miami Open.

No one on Tour had played as many matches in 2019. The shoulder, despite public assurances, clearly was a concern.

But when you're winning the way Andreescu was winning, you don't ever want to stop.

And so she played. And in the first round, she ran into...Irina-Camelia Begu, for the second tournament in a row.

Andreescu caught a break when the match was postponed for 24 hours because of rain. Still, it wasn't nearly enough time to recover.

The transition from the unusually cool conditions in the desert to the heat and humidity in Miami, where the tournament had relocated from breezy Key Biscayne to the asphalt parking lot of Hard Rock Stadium adjacent to the Florida Turnpike, was a challenge.

Andreescu's shoulder was still taped. And she was using the ice towel, and ice bags, and pouring bottles of water over her head to try to stay cool.

Once again, the Canadian lost the first set. And she was down 1-4 in the second set. Once again, she would have to come back.

She was in tears as Bruneau took the court.

"I'm not feeling anything out there. Every time I try to do the right thing, it never goes my way," she told him. "I'm getting so mad at myself. I'm, like, so irritated."

From 1-5, Andreescu brought it to 5-5, and won the second-set tiebreak—and the match.

By the time Andreescu got to the Miami Open, her shoulder was painful and her arm was heavily taped.

The body was protesting mightily, but the spirit just kept winning.

In the second round, Andreescu avenged her Acapulco loss to Kenin by defeating her in straight sets.

And the reality of her new circumstances was beginning to kick in.

After that win, she was besieged by a horde of autograph- and selfie-seekers.

"They were pretty aggressive," Andreescu said after the match.

And then—another rematch. This time it was a replay of the Indian Wells final less than a week before, against Kerber.

The result was the same, a 6-4, 4-6, 6-1 victory for Andreescu that had the German lefty spitting nails at the net during the briefest of handshakes.

If there was palm contact, it was fleeting. If there was eye contact, it was accidental.

"You're the biggest drama queen ever," Kerber hissed over the roar of the crowd.

Players don't generally appreciate it when their opponents get on-court treatment, look as though it's all just too much—only to come back out on court when the points start and compete as though nothing was amiss.

But it happens; the best in the world do a great job in putting aside the physical nicks that all of them have, and play on regardless.

Andreescu still had the strapping on her shoulder, with tape running down her right arm and another bandage below the elbow—with the hair band over that, of course.

She had a medical timeout during the match to try to loosen her shoulder. And she had the additional allowed two visits limited to the 90-second changeover time for more treatment.

In other words, nothing illegal or even out of the ordinary.

But the 31-year-old Kerber clearly was out of sorts after back-to-back defeats to an upstart 18-year-old.

You could hardly blame her. And yet, she was in good company.

Andreescu was now 31–3 on the season.

But the streak would end when the shoulder said *no más* during her fourth-round match against Anett Kontaveit of Estonia.

Andreescu retired down 0-6, 1-2.

Her run was over.

As spring arrived back home in Canada, she was now No. 23 in the world, and officially in the big leagues. ●

Drama Queen! Losing twice in a week to a teenager didn't sit well with former world No. 1 Angelique Kerber. (Photo: AP Images)

THE GOOD-LUCK CHARM

The accessory that has become her trademark was a random accident.

And now, given the incredible 2019 Bianca Andreescu had, she goes nowhere and doesn't hit a single tennis ball without the coiled hair elastic positioned just above her right elbow.

She wore the elastic for her season-opening tournament in Auckland, New Zealand. And after going from the qualifying, beating two former No. 1s and reaching the final, there was no point in tempting fate.

"I have never worn these hair ties before. But during preseason I bought a couple, and I was just wearing it around my wrist. And then I was noticing that when I was hitting forehands it kept flying off, so I just put it up (above the elbow), and it looked decent, so I just kept it," Andreescu said during a press conference at Indian Wells in March.

"I like to be different. So I guess I'm starting a bit of a trend, because a lot of people actually have messaged me about it saying they're wearing it now too. So it's pretty nice."

Andreescu now has them in all sorts of colours, after the manufacturer sent her a supply.

And she wears them no matter what else she's wearing.

If it's a long-sleeved pullover, she often wears it over the sleeve.

If she has some taping on the arm, as has been the case at times this season, she just slips it on right over the tape.

The only question left unanswered: what does the tan line look like?

PAIN IN PARIS, TRIUMPH IN TORONTO

In the wake of the injury-scarred exit in Miami, it was a foregone conclusion that Bianca Andreescu would withdraw from a planned participation in the Volvo Open, a Premier-level WTA tournament in picturesque Charleston, South Carolina, slated for early April.

But the Canadian who was always so proud to play for her country also had to pull out of a crucial Fed Cup tie against the Czech Republic in Prostejov later in the month.

Andreescu had won both her singles matches to clinch a playoff tie against the Netherlands in February. That victory earned Canada the right to play in April for a promotion into Group I, composed of the top eight nations in women's tennis.

The previous year against Ukraine in Montreal, she had teamed up with Gabriela Dabrowski in doubles to clinch the victory that kept Canada in Group II, in position to compete for the top group in 2019.

In that tie against Ukraine, Andreescu had been pressed into emergency service on the first day when teammate Françoise Abanda took a spill in her pre-match warmup and hit her head—hard—on the court.

Andreescu had come through for Team Canada in February, so she was disappointed to have to miss a big Fed Cup match against the Czech Republic in April because of the shoulder.

Andreescu is rolled off court in a wheelchair after suffering cramps during a Fed Cup tie vs. Ukraine in February 2019.

Andreescu already had enjoyed a full breakfast. She was ready to settle in for the day and cheer on her teammates when she got the 11th-hour call.

Without a proper warmup or any preparation at all, Andreescu took the court and gave Ukraine No. 1 Lesia Tsurenko everything she could handle—until a calf cramp felled her in the third set.

She was rolled off the court in a wheelchair.

But Andreescu returned the following day, with the calf heavily taped and far from 100 percent, to seal the win for Canada in the fifth and deciding match after teammate Genie Bouchard had posted two impressive singles victories.

The tie against the Czechs was the reward, the opportunity she had pushed herself to the limit for.

But after 35 matches in three months, and with the shoulder a major concern, she couldn't risk jeopardizing the rest of her season.

So she regretfully had to bow out.

Without Andreescu or Bouchard, an understaffed Canadian squad was swept, 4-0.

A Return in Paris?

Andreescu had targeted her return for the French Open at the end of May. And she did everything she could to make that date.

Before heading to Paris, she travelled to the Rafa Nadal Academy in Mallorca to get some repetitions in on the red clay, to see if the shoulder would hold up, and to gauge whether she could withstand the rigors of her first French Open main draw.

The training week was chosen over the alternative, which was to play a warmup tournament the week before. But the practice was judged more valuable than match play. And when Andreescu arrived in Paris, she pronounced herself pain-free.

It was a tight timeline, but she made it.

In retrospect, it might have been *too* tight.

It didn't help that Andreescu's first opponent was a stubborn retriever from the Czech Republic, qualifier Marie Bouzkova.

And it helped even less that the earlier matches that day ran long. Andreescu and Bouzkova were halted after two sets because of darkness.

When they resumed the next afternoon, Andreescu pulled out a 5-7, 6-4, 6-4 victory that took three hours over the two days and clearly extracted a toll.

"I'm not going to lie. This wasn't one of my best matches at all. I was getting pretty mad at myself," Andreescu said in her post-match press conference. "But, I mean, it's my first tournament back after an injury, so I tried to stay as calm as possible. And I'm just really proud of how I fought through the match with the tennis I had."

Andreescu downplayed the state of her shoulder.

Over two days and more than three hours on court, Andreescu's return to play in her French Open main draw debut resulted in a victory.

"I was a little bit sore today. I'm not surprised because it's my first match in six weeks (actually, it was just over two months). All the nerves are kicking in again. But I got treatment and I'm feeling really good actually—considering," she said. "Shoulder, it's really good and I'm really pleased. Just got to keep getting treatment and I'll be good."

Unfortunately, the carryover meant that Andreescu wouldn't enjoy the normal Grand Slam day off between rounds. And in the second round she was to face a familiar foe in American Sofia Kenin.

It was shaping up to be another marathon, especially on the slower red clay surface.

Despite all her bravado, it was therefore no surprise that Andreescu withdrew from the tournament.

Clearly, it was too soon. And no one knew when she would return.

Except that when she did, the shoulder would be right.

It had to be.

As the rest of the players were taking part in grass-court warmup tournaments and getting ready for Wimbledon, Andreescu flew to Arizona to be evaluated by noted physical therapist Todd Ellenbecker, vice-president of medical services for the men's ATP Tour.

She made some minor technical adjustments to take pressure off the shoulder on the serve. And—perhaps most importantly—she was able to hop off the speed train for a little while, to rest body and mind after a frantic start to the season.

"I changed my fitness regimen. I think that was the main thing. I started to do a lot more shoulder exercises and shoulder rehab on a daily basis, because I felt like it was weak," Andreescu said in Toronto on the eve of the Rogers Cup in early August.

"I'd been playing so many matches for the first three months of the year, and I felt all that was catching up to me at Indian Wells."

Andreescu said that there was a bit of a biomechanical issue, so she did modify "bits and pieces on the serve."

It wasn't by choice, but Andreescu was to enjoy a luxury that few players have in the middle of the infernally long tennis season: a chance to recover, refuel, and regain some of the fitness lost during tournament play.

The Queen of Toronto

The Rogers Cup is a major tournament. And as it was on rotation in Toronto in 2019, with Andreescu's star most definitely on the rise, the teenager was set to be the big hometown attraction.

Andreescu and Marie Bouzkova of the Czech Republic would both shine at the Rogers Cup later that summer.

There was doubt until the very last minute about whether Andreescu would be ready for her first main draw appearance at the Rogers Cup.

But in the end, she answered the bell.

Had it been any other tournament, it's entirely possible Andreescu might have skipped the Rogers Cup altogether.

In the end, the decision was made to play. Andreescu said it was "borderline."

But after playing only one match in the four and a half months leading up to the tournament, expectations had to be tempered even if the Canadian said she was feeling very good.

"I would say 12 out of 10, really. I haven't felt this strong in a while. I had a really good, I guess, sort of mini-preseason where I was able to focus a lot on my physique and just focus on other aspects of my game," she said. "And not only that, but on me as a person, too. I think I really improved a lot of things. So I'm really grateful for that break, and I think all that preparation is paying off."

After her marathon first-round win in Paris, Andreescu had insisted her shoulder felt great. Two days later, she pulled out of the tournament. So while the positivity had to be taken with a grain of salt, the proof would be displayed on court.

The draw gods were not kind. Andreescu's first-round opponent was to be her immediate predecessor as the queen of Canadian women's tennis, Genie Bouchard.

"I definitely looked up to her growing up because she was the only (Canadian) woman tennis player who was on the tour at the time," Andreescu said.

The two also had been teammates, representing their country in Fed Cup play.

There was a certain irony to the matchup. The last time the WTA Tour stopped in Toronto, in 2017, right after Andreescu's breakout debut in Washington, D.C., Bouchard had somewhat flippantly offered to "pass the torch" to Andreescu after her first-round loss to Donna Vekic of Croatia.

"She's a good player. So someone else can carry the burden of Canada," Bouchard said of Andreescu in comments that went viral.

Meanwhile, Andreescu admitted she was feeling the weight of expectations.

"I feel that. I'm not going to lie. I'm usually pretty good with stuff like that, I try not to get too overwhelmed," she said. "But yeah, there is some pressure. You're playing at home. This is my first tournament back as well. At this point, I'm just really happy to be back on court, and I'm going to give it my all."

The younger Canadian began slowly against Bouchard, shaking off a little rust and peppering the stadium court at the Aviva Centre with errors.

It was a tough draw for both as Andreescu met Genie Bouchard, the player she had replaced as the Canadian No. 1, in the first round in the Rogers Cup in Toronto. (Photo: AP Images)

Despite having played just one match since March, Andreescu won six straight matches—three of them against top-10 players—to win her hometown Rogers Cup. (Photo: AP Images)

Bouchard, the former No. 5 and 2014 Wimbledon finalist who had not won a main draw match on the WTA Tour since February, had been comprehensively beaten by her young countrywoman at the smaller event in Newport Beach, California, in January. But she looked in vintage form to start the match, and won the first set.

Andreescu found her range. And in the end, she pulled off a comeback victory of the sort that was becoming her trademark.

"In the first set I was a bit nervous. But I shook off those nerves, and I tried to refocus for the second set. And I stuck to the right tactics. I made sure to put pressure right from the start of the point," Andreescu said. "I think things just switched on for me in the second set. I started going for my shots more and that really helped."

More importantly, she said the shoulder felt fine. And as Andreescu went through the week, facing quality opponents at every stage, it continued to feel fine.

She strained her groin during the match against Bouchard, and the familiar leg wrap reappeared. But Andreescu pulled off another comeback victory the next day against Russia's Daria Kasatkina, who plays a similar style of tennis.

In the third round, she upset world No. 5 Kiki Bertens of the Netherlands—again in three sets. Twenty-four hours later, it was No.

3 Karolina Pliskova's turn to be dispatched— yes, in three sets.

Four consecutive days, 12 sets of tennis, and Andreescu was gathering steam.

Her semifinal opponent was a familiar foe: once again, as she had earlier in the season in Acapulco and Miami, she would play Sofia Kenin.

Andreescu also had been due to face Kenin again in the second round of the French Open before she withdrew.

This one was a straight-set, if tight, victory for Andreescu.

On the sixth consecutive day, in the final, Andreescu would face an icon.

The Problem with Serena...

The positive for Andreescu in her first career match against the legendary Serena Williams was that she would be on home turf.

And the Toronto tennis fans, normally a placid lot, had energized and gotten fully behind their native daughter this year.

The downside? With the loss of only one set in the tournament, Williams had been looking very, very dangerous.

Since her return from the birth of daughter Olympia, the 37-year-old had yet to complete a full tournament outside the Grand Slams.

But with the knee issue from the spring behind her, it appeared the Rogers Cup would break that pattern.

Andreescu and Williams bonded at the Rogers Cup. They would soon meet again. (Photo: AP Images)

Unbeknownst to Andreescu—or anyone outside the tight inner circle—Williams had felt back spasms during her semifinal victory over qualifier Marie Bouzkova, in which she had lost the first set 6-1.

The American had suffered them before. She had all the treatment she could. "Hours and hours of treatment," she said afterward.

Had it not been a final, she might well have ceded a walkover.

But Williams did take the court, saying later she "hoped for a miracle."

But it was clear from the first point, as her feet appeared encased in cement, that she wasn't right.

The legs were fine physically, just frozen from stress and nerves.

The back, not so fine.

At 3-1 in the first set, Williams headed for her chair even though it was not time for a change of ends.

It wasn't long before it was over.

And in the aftermath, Andreescu's handling of the situation made news well beyond the small bubble of the tennis world.

"Can I Hug You?"

The Canadian kneeled down in front of Williams, asked if she could give her a hug, and gave a superstar old enough to be her mother all the comfort she could, from the bottom of her queen-sized heart.

In a rare show of on-court emotion, Williams couldn't hold back the tears.

They were like two best girlfriends sharing a moment—oblivious to the 10,000 fans in the stands, and perhaps millions more watching around the world.

But in the end Andreescu, improbably, had won the Rogers Cup.

Even if it wasn't how she had visualized it.

"The win in Indian Wells was—I mean, it was a hard-fought battle. So I felt like it was a sweeter victory at the time," Andreescu said. "But this tournament is at home. I've dedicated so much hard work and sweat on that tennis court and in this gym, so this tournament is definitely 10 times more special."

For Williams, the moment was bittersweet. But she had nothing but praise for her young rival.

"I think Bianca is a great girl, always have. That's why I have always wanted to play her. She's just a fabulous personality. She's...an old soul," Williams said.

"I'm officially a fan—I mean, I was before, like I said. But I just think I was really sad, and she made me feel a lot better, so that was really nice," she added. "She definitely doesn't seem like a 19-year-old in her words, on court, and her game, her attitude, her actions."

With the title, Andreescu rose from No. 27 in the world to No. 14 and officially became a contender for the US Open title.

The icon and the "old soul" would both arrive in New York two weeks later, officially rivals, but having created a new and rather heartwarming bond. ●

"Can I hug you?" Andreescu consoles Williams after she retired from their match at the Rogers Cup final. (Photo: AP Images)

A DREAM RUN AT FLUSHING MEADOWS

6

After her monumental hometown victory at the Rogers Cup, Bianca Andreescu wisely chose to bow out of the Western & Southern Open in Cincinnati, Ohio, the following week.

It was a tournament every bit as prestigious as the one in Toronto, with significant prize money and ranking points at stake. But if Andreescu had learned anything from the attempted Indian Wells–Miami double back in March, it was the importance of listening to her body.

With the final Grand Slam of the season looming and expectations growing, health was paramount.

So she arrived in noisy, bustling New York City still riding a wave of confidence, the mind and body both rested.

Andreescu was going to need every bit of energy she could store.

Because suddenly, in the first US Open main draw of her young career, Andreescu wasn't merely seeded No. 15.

She was regularly included in the pre-tournament predictions as a player who not

Pomp and circumstance on full display inside Arthur Ashe Stadium during the 2019 US Open.

only could make a deep run—but maybe could even go all the way.

A Popular New Attraction

Her first practice on Court 13 at the Billie Jean King National Tennis Center the Thursday before the tournament drew an impressive crowd, even though it was after 7 p.m. and the fans on hand to watch the qualifying rounds had been there since morning.

The next day, Andreescu was among the select players invited to the "Media Day" event, held inside cavernous Louis Armstrong Stadium. The top players give their pre-

Andreescu has a little fun as she gets her first look inside cavernous Arthur Ashe Stadium.

tournament press conferences and television interviews on this day and, for the second year, fans were invited to attend.

They come not so much to listen to what the players might say as to catch an autograph or selfie as they leave the stadium. It's noisy and a little chaotic at times.

She wasn't a top seed, or even an American. But there Andreescu was up on the stage, answering questions about her odds of winning the tournament.

On Sunday, the eve of opening day, Andreescu and Serena Williams happened to be practicing on neighboring courts.

As Williams left, she walked behind Andreescu, who was going through the paces with her hitting partner.

They acknowledged each other, displaying none of the intimacy that had been so heartwarmingly on display just two weeks before after the aborted Toronto final.

There was no way to know, then, that the tennis gods would decree they'd meet again in 13 days—out of the 128 women who started the tournament, the last two still standing.

Somewhere deep down, being in opposite halves of the 128-player draw, could either have an inkling it might happen?

We'll never know. But tennis players tend not to look too far into the future. They learn the dangers of overlooking the present at a very young age, usually through the hard knocks of personal experience.

There was a long, winding road to travel before the 19-year-old rookie—or even the 37-year-old six-time champion—could contemplate the possibility of lifting the trophy.

Williams, the biggest star in the women's draw, was chasing tennis immortality at her home-country Grand Slam tournament.

In her 20th US Open, she was featured in cavernous Arthur Ashe Stadium Monday night, in a highly anticipated clash of superstars against Maria Sharapova.

Andreescu's US Open debut was significantly more modest.

On Tuesday afternoon, she was scheduled on Court 10—a nice court, but the ninth-largest match court on the grounds with a capacity of 1,104.

She met American Katie Volynets, a wild-card entrant 18 months younger who competed in the junior event the following week.

Andreescu was visibly tense, her legs dotted with square patches covering up what she later said were "bites." She also had tape

That early practice paid off as Andreescu returned later to beat former No. 1 Caroline Wozniacki for the second time in 2019.

Thigh wrapped, knee wrapped, Andreescu starts her US Open campaign.

below her left knee, which she said had been bothering her in practice.

She was facing a younger opponent—a new experience. She hadn't played an official match for a few weeks. And she was coming into her first US Open main draw with surprising pressure and expectations.

"I know she's American, but hopefully I can get the crowd support, as well," Andreescu said of the opponent she had defeated 6-2, 7-6 on her way to that title in Newport Beach, California, earlier in the season.

Sometimes, it's a matter of just getting through that first match so that those pre-tournament jitters—those worst-case scenario, negative thoughts—can be replaced by adrenaline and ambition.

And Andreescu did just that, defeating Volynets 6-2, 6-4.

There were a lot of winners, and even more errors. She struggled on second serve. She didn't display her entire arsenal of shots. But she won.

Andreescu was surprised to find a huge contingent of fans—Canadians, and new Andreescu fans—cheering her on. There were maple leafs and red-and-white attire all around the court, which was standing-room only.

"I loved it. These Canadians are wilding," she said in her press conference.

Next up was another challenge, one of a more cerebral nature against 33-year-old Belgian veteran Kirsten Flipkens.

A Tactical Battle

Not a power player, Flipkens brings a similar approach to the court as Andreescu does. She changes the pace, uses her slice, comes to the net—in a nutshell, her game is to take her opponent out of her rhythm, put her in uncomfortable positions, and earn her points any number of ways.

That's exactly what Andreescu likes to do, although she adds a significant power component.

After shaking off some early nerves, Andreescu dispatched American teenager Katie Volynets in the first round.

So the matchup—a first between the two—was an intriguing one.

The Canadian won it 6-3, 7-5. It was a high-quality affair in which both players attacked the net. But Andreescu cleaned up her game considerably from the first round, notably cutting down on the unforced errors.

After the match, Flipkens had nothing but praise.

"I told her that it was a good match and that I think she can win this tournament, so she should believe in her capabilities," Flipkens said. "She really played well. And if you win Toronto, Indian Wells, it's almost the same status as a Grand Slam."

They played on Court 5, a similarly sized court to Court 10.

But as Andreescu reached the third round of a Grand Slam for the first time, her court fortunes were about to improve considerably.

The Big Stage

For her third-round match against former world No. 1 and US Open finalist Caroline Wozniacki, Andreescu would make her Arthur Ashe Stadium debut.

The massive arena, opened in 1997 with a roof added in 2016, seats 23,771. If you're up in the top rows, it can be difficult to distinguish one player from another—especially if they're clothed by the same sponsor.

Down on the court, you have to resist the temptation to look up, and up, and up, and risk being awed by the sheer scale and dimensions of it.

The morning of the match, Andreescu had an opportunity to practice inside the stadium her next opponent had competed on countless times during a 15-year pro career.

She took to the court just as 15-year-old American phenomenon Coco Gauff was leaving. With the maturity of her 19 years, the Canadian went right over to introduce herself; the present and future met...the future.

"I told her, 'Congrats on all the success. Keep killing it. NextGen is here!'" Andreescu recounted.

The victory over Wozniacki was another straight-set affair, 6-4, 6-4. Still more errors than winners. But Wozniacki didn't appear 100 percent healthy, which helped. Regardless, Andreescu dealt with the atmosphere at Ashe Stadium as though it was just a routine day at the office.

It didn't feel that way when she first walked on the court, though.

"I was, like, 'Oh my god, is this actually happening right now?' It's a dream come true,

Andreescu enjoyed plenty of support from Canadian fans during the early rounds of the US Open.

so I prepared myself really well. I handled my emotions well today," Andreescu said.

Andreescu had defeated Wozniacki, then No. 3 in the world, at the Auckland tournament in January. Back then, she shocked everyone, including herself.

Eight months later, now ranked ahead of the Dane, there was little shocking about it.

Battling an American— In Her Back Yard

Having conquered Arthur Ashe Stadium, Andreescu's next challenge would be to conquer a partisan—and very well-refreshed— Arthur Ashe Stadium night-match crowd.

Meanwhile, American Taylor Townsend was having a breakthrough US Open that included a major victory in the second round.

The 23-year-old upset No. 4 seed Simona Halep in a third-set tiebreaker to earn the round-of-16 meeting with Andreescu.

And that was a break.

The child of Romanian parents, Andreescu had always looked up to Halep as a role model. And the reigning Wimbledon champion had been kind and encouraging, in their brief interactions.

A meeting with Halep, in a big stadium, with a Grand Slam quarterfinal spot on the line, could have been a daunting proposition for the Canadian rookie.

Instead, she faced Townsend, who also was in her first quarterfinal.

The American posed challenges of her own, though. She is like no other player on the WTA Tour.

Townsend is left-handed. And she's a rare player who serves-and-volleys on a regular basis. Even her pre-match warmup is different; Townsend starts at the net with volleys. No one else does that. And in a sport where so many are creatures of habit, it can be off-putting even if it's perfectly legal.

"Simona (Halep) surely took her seriously, but didn't have the advantage we had, knowing Taylor was playing very well, and especially in beating Simona," Andreescu coach Sylvain Bruneau said. "With her technique, Bianca is very comfortable with players who come to the net. She can come over the ball, make it dip quickly, go for angles, and she likes having a target."

Andreescu handled the challenge with aplomb in a 6-1, 4-6, 6-2 victory that put her into the elite eight.

For the uninitiated, night matches in Arthur Ashe Stadium can be like an alternate universe.

The new roof shuts in the sounds, which echo around the massive building. The air circulation patterns were changed by the $500 million roof addition, making the conditions especially humid and clammy.

Andreescu and countrywoman Sharon Fichman lost their first-round doubles match. But Andreescu got a good look at her quarterfinal singles opponent, American Taylor Townsend.

"Bianca really likes having the crowd for her, and last night was tough love—no love, even. That's okay; it's part of the things that she needs to learn to deal with, to surmount," Bruneau said. "It wasn't easy, but she got there."

A Nice Draw

If Halep, one of Andreescu's role models, had been eliminated before the two could meet, two more serious US Open contenders also had been ousted early in the tournament.

No. 11 seed Sloane Stephens, the 2017 US Open champion and another American, went out meekly in the first round to Russia's Anna Kalinskaya.

And No. 6 seed Petra Kvitova of the Czech Republic, whose power makes it a major challenge for a player like Andreescu to execute her game, went out in the second round.

And so, rather than one of those two stars, Andreescu had to defeat No. 25 seed Elise Mertens to get to the semifinal.

Arthur Ashe Stadium court is immense, but Andreescu was well used to it by the time she reached the final against Serena Williams.

Mertens is a powerful server, a smooth mover, and a top player who ended up winning the women's doubles event with Aryna Sabalenka of Belarus. But she's not a Grand Slam champion.

The 24-year-old from Belgium could not put a foot wrong in the first set. But Andreescu—a master of comebacks in this astonishing breakout season—pulled off another one in a 3-6, 6-2, 6-3 victory.

It was another night match in Ashe—but without the atmosphere that reigned during the match against Townsend.

Mertens is largely unknown to American audiences. And Andreescu had most of the neutrals.

Still, once she closed out the match, she looked incredulous as she gazed up to her group of supporters.

"I said, 'Is this real life?' Twice. I couldn't really believe it at that moment. But then when I sat down, I just couldn't stop smiling, like I can't now," she said after the match. "If someone told me that I was going to be in the semifinal of the US Open a year ago, I would say, 'You're crazy.' So I'm just really proud of myself with how I dealt (with being) injured. I kept that passion going."

Mertens acknowledged the younger Andreescu's competitive skill.

"She's still young, no pressure. I think if you can serve well at the big moments, you can do well at the big moments. That's maybe something she does very well," she said. "Also get that one more strike. She's a very powerful hitter but also a good mover."

Trying Not to Look Ahead

The Grand Slam schedule is a friendly one to a player who is managing injuries.

And let's face it, rare is the player who isn't—especially at the business end of a Grand Slam tournament and after eight gruelling months on the tennis circuit.

But in New York, Andreescu had an off day between each of her first six matches. And the addition of a full-time physiotherapist/osteopath to the team, the experienced Austrian Kirstin Bauer, in the spring clearly was paying dividends.

By the time Andreescu faced Mertens, the tape under the left knee was gone.

By the semifinal clash with No. 13 seed Belinda Bencic, the wrap high up on her right thigh that had first appeared in the second round against Flipkens also was gone.

The shoulder, so problematic through the summer, continued to be problem-free.

"I think it is really helping me physically because I haven't been having any pain whatsoever throughout this whole tournament," Andreescu said of the addition of Bauer.

But the quarterfinal match against Mertens was on Wednesday night. The semifinal against Bencic was on Thursday night. So that extra recovery time wasn't on the menu for this one.

Andreescu's Swiss opponent was only 22, but it felt as though Bencic had been around forever.

She was just 16 when she reached the quarterfinal at her first US Open in 2014. This was her fifth; she missed three of the four majors in 2017 because of injury.

Bencic's early career was overseen by Melanie Molitor, the mother of Swiss legend Martina Hingis. And the traces of Hingis' craftiness and guile were evident in her game.

After peaking at No. 7 in the rankings at age 18, and climbing all the way back from an injury-induced rock bottom of No. 318 after the 2017 US Open, she had been playing the best tennis of her career.

In the fourth round, Bencic had eliminated defending champion and No. 1 seed Naomi Osaka in straight sets.

If there was a difference between the two on this night, it was how Andreescu refused to cede in the key moments.

She converted 4-of-7 break-point opportunities on Bencic's serve. And she saved 10-of-13 break points on her own serve in a 7-6 (3), 7-5 victory that, at two hours and 13 minutes, was her longest of the tournament to that point.

Andreescu won just eight more points than Bencic did. If you subtract the nine double faults from her unforced error tally, a by-product of her being bold with her second serve, the Canadian played a highly aggressive match while keeping the free points to a relative minimum.

"I've always dreamt of this moment ever since I was a little kid. But I don't think many people would have actually thought that it would become a reality," Andreescu said. "I think that moment after the match, I was just in shock. At the same time, I fought really hard to get to this point. So I really think I deserve to be in the final on Saturday."

Only one match remained—the biggest challenge of Andreescu's young tennis career, against a woman twice her age chasing tennis immortality on her own home turf.

It was a rematch of the Rogers Cup final. But the circumstances couldn't have been more different, the stakes any higher.

Regardless of the outcome, it was not going to end after four games this time. ●

There was plenty of buzz around Andreescu coming into New York, even though she wasn't one of the top seeds. She held her own press conference on Media Day before the event.

7

A FINAL FOR (TWO) AGES

At 37, shortly to turn 38, the legendary Serena Williams had nothing left to prove after an illustrious career that has her on the cusp of tennis immortality.

She has 23 Grand Slam singles titles, one fewer than the Australian Margaret Court.

But in the endless debate about the meaning of those numbers, it's often pointed out that Court won 11 of those 23 major titles at the Australian Open during an era when the tournament was very much a country cousin to the other three Grand Slam tournaments.

What is now the traditional January Grand Slam opener was held in December back then. And many top players from Europe and North America routinely skipped the infernally long trip Down Under to spend the holidays with their loved ones and play lucrative, low-pressure exhibition matches instead.

All of which is to say, Williams' status as the all-time great in the women's game is cemented in the minds of almost everyone.

Still, the champion's fire remains undimmed. The drive that gets you to 23 cannot be extinguished on command, like blowing out a match.

Having returned in March 2018 after being out 14 months through pregnancy, the birth of daughter Olympia, and some major post-birth complications, she was motivated in a different way.

Bianca Andreescu, 19, and Serena Williams, 37, pose for a photo before their singles final at the 2019 US Open.

And yet, through three previous Grand Slam singles finals since her return, Williams had appeared hamstrung both by physical woes and by the late-career nerves that have shackled many a brilliant athlete at a similar age.

Outside the majors, Williams had not even properly finished a tournament in intermittent play in 2019. Withdrawals and mid-match retirements were becoming the new standard.

Williams retired from her match at Indian Wells. She withdrew in Rome before facing sister Venus. And she cut short the Rogers Cup final against Andreescu after just four games.

A year ago, in the same Arthur Ashe Stadium, Williams met young Japanese rising star Naomi Osaka in her quest for No. 24. It ended in defeat amid dramatic circumstances that gained worldwide attention far beyond the confines of the tennis world.

This time, she was determined to create a different outcome.

Healthy and Fit, At Last

The women's singles final is the main match on the second Saturday of the US Open.

So unlike earlier in the tournament when the fans tend to trickle into massive Arthur Ashe Stadium, almost everyone was in their seats from the first serve.

Nearly all were fervently hoping Williams could make history, and they could say they saw it live.

Williams takes a look at her new friend after a practice session before the start of the US Open. Two weeks later, they'd cross paths again.

Williams had looked much like her old self through the fortnight. At least, as close to that level as she had since her comeback 18 months before.

She, too, skipped the Cincinnati event after the injury retirement in Toronto. But the American had shown no sign of any issues through six victories.

"When you play a Grand Slam final, there is a lot of emotion. When you play for a record like this one, there is even more, which is fine. It's called pressure, and I think Serena had to experience a bit of pressure in her life. And you can't think that she's not good dealing with pressure," Williams coach Patrick Mouratoglou said. "But if you feel weak or not as strong as you wish you would, it's more difficult to beat the pressure. When you don't move well, you can't be as confident as you should be, because if your 'A' game doesn't work, you don't have any other option, and for me that's what happened."

Mouratoglou added that since the knee issues she suffered during the French Open in May had been resolved by Wimbledon, Williams was moving better than she had since her return in March 2018.

For her tournament opener against Maria Sharapova, Williams was as pumped up as if it were the final.

She destroyed her longtime rival—who's not a true rival on the court, as Williams leads their head-to-head series 20–2—with the loss of only two games.

And after one hiccup in the first set of her second-round match against 17-year-old American Caty McNally, she had rolled through the rest of her opponents.

Williams' 6-3, 6-1 win over No. 5 seed Elina Svitolina in the semifinal was comprehensive.

There seemed to be no physical issues. Her legendary serve was firing.

Would this be the day to finally put Grand Slam title No. 24 in the books?

Winning Is a Habit

Meanwhile, Andreescu hadn't lost a completed match since...February.

That was when Kenin defeated her in the semifinal of a smaller tournament in Acapulco, Mexico, the week before Indian Wells.

Since then, notwithstanding the long periods of inactivity because of her shoulder injury, Andreescu had won 22 matches and lost only one. After the shocking victory at the BNP Paribas Open in Indian Wells, California, she retired because of the shoulder early in the second set against Anett Kontaveit in the fourth round of the Miami Open the next week.

In sharp contrast to the pro-Andreescu crowd at Rogers Cup, the Arthur Ashe Stadium crowd was vociferously behind Williams in her quest to make tennis history.

When all you've done is win, it's exponentially easier to eradicate any thoughts of losing from your mind.

Mouratoglou, who also had accurately predicted Russia's Daniil Medvedev would reach the men's singles final, wasn't surprised to see Andreescu on the other side of the net.

"I expected her in the final, and I think she's going to be No. 1 in the future, because she has everything that's needed to be No. 1. A lot of respect for her," he said. "She has the whole package. Like, the game's amazing, I think: the physical, the athleticism, and the mental. She looks incredibly confident. She feels like she's where she belongs. That's the impression she gives."

Asked what she would have said if someone told her a year ago, when she limped out of the qualifying in New York in the first round, that she would be playing Serena Williams in the singles final 12 months later, Andreescu's response was two-fold.

"I don't think I would have believed them. I was ranked, like, outside the top 150, I think. It's just crazy what a year can do," she said. "If someone would have said that a couple weeks ago, I think I *would* have believed them."

But this was Serena Williams.

The legend.

The "beast," as Andreescu had affectionately called her in Toronto.

But once again, just as in her three previous Grand Slam finals, the beast did not appear on this late Saturday afternoon in Queens.

Williams surrendered the first game of the match to Andreescu by double-faulting two consecutive times, from deuce.

She would mimic her serve motion, her face a study in anguish and despair, and bemoan her inability to maximize her greatest weapon.

And yet, she was unable to loosen up enough to figure out the problem and fix it, find her reliable, powerful motion once again.

Without it, she was not the same player.

To give credit where due, the fearless Andreescu had a lot to do with that. Her aggressiveness in attacking Williams' second serve put even more pressure on that wavering first delivery.

From the start, the Canadian stood right at the baseline. And it was Serena who had to back off a bit to handle what was coming at her.

To win points, Williams was having to hit outright winners, again and again. Unless

In her first major final, the teenaged Andreescu displayed the poise of an experienced veteran.

you've having a day when everything goes right, that's not a winning formula.

If Mouratoglou was confident his charge was finally ready physically, it became evident that emotionally, the same doubts continued to plague her.

Meanwhile, the Canadian showed no outward signs of being overwhelmed by the situation.

The moments she shared with Williams on court in Toronto, after Williams retired with the back issue and shed tears as Andreescu went over to comfort her, may well have demystified the legend in an intangible but significant way.

She saw the impenetrable champion in a vulnerable moment, up close and personal. And perhaps that helped peel away a layer or two of armor and allowed Andreescu to understand that a player she had up on a pedestal was, in reality, just another human being.

The experience the Canadian gained facing the somewhat hostile crowd in the win over Townsend earlier in the tournament came in very handy when it came to shutting out a crowd fervently urging Williams on at an even higher decibel level.

As Andreescu took the first set, the pro-Serena crowd was even cheering when Andreescu missed a first serve.

Williams anxiously mimics her service motion, on a day when her greatest weapon completely deserted her.

If the crowd erupted in applause when she double-faulted, she shut it out. When the crowd stood as one to give Williams an ovation for merely winning her serve game, Andreescu didn't hear it.

By the beginning of the second set, Williams was gesturing to her team and family—including HRH the Duchess of Sussex, a close friend—beseeching them for help they couldn't provide.

One Final Stand

The Canadian was up 6-3, 5-1 and on her way to an improbably routine victory when Williams made one last champion's stand.

As Andreescu said afterward, that was to be expected from a legend.

She expected it. Which didn't make it any easier to stop the streak of four consecutive games lost, including two when she served for the title.

The crowd, stunned at times, was just waiting for another opportunity to explode.

As Williams evened the second set at 5-5, that was the opportunity for Cinderella Bianca to let the clock strike midnight. It was the moment when she could succumb to the undertow of history.

No one would have thought less of Andreescu's effort. In these early days of her

Andreescu reacts after winning the US Open. (Photo: AP Images)

career, failing to accomplish the unexpected is a forgivable offence.

But for Williams, that dynamic is reversed. With her sterling résumé, she's rarely forgiven for failing to do the expected.

Perhaps she doesn't even forgive herself.

But it turned out that was all the fight Williams had left.

Whatever game plan she and Mouratoglou had fashioned before the match, it wasn't working. And Williams' on-court brain wasn't thinking lucidly enough to try something different, conjure up other ways to stop her teenaged opponent.

It seemed as though she just kept waiting for her own game to click in, for her legendary serve to return. But that never happened.

Seeing the finish line, Andreescu smoothly stepped across it as though she'd been doing it her entire career.

She dropped her racket, embraced a smiling Williams at the net, and fell to the court, lying flat on her back.

It's a pose tennis fans have seen from men's legend Rafael Nadal during many of his 19 Grand Slam triumphs.

For the Canadian, in her first of what could be many such triumphs, it looked as though she were making snow angels.

All of the experience Andreescu had gained through a season of near-constant winning came together for this unforgettable moment.

As she climbed into the stands, a stepladder magically appearing for precisely that purpose, her support staff and family awaited.

Andreescu's embrace with parents Maria and Nicu was a moment to melt even the coldest heart.

For a decade, more than half her young life, they had persevered as a family, making whatever sacrifices were necessary in pursuit of this dream.

For some tennis families, this moment never comes. For the Andreescus, it came so early in their daughter's career as to be far beyond anything they could ever have imagined. ●

Left: After withstanding one last, furious stand by Williams, Andreescu was on the cusp of a championship. Opposite: Andreescu hugs mother Maria and father Nicu in the stands, after winning her first career Grand Slam title.

THE POWER OF THE MIND

At the top level of tennis, where every player is enormously talented, it's the intangibles that can make the difference between winning and losing.

And Bianca Andreescu is fully engaged in exploring all the benefits that come with working to control the mind, and not just the body.

She does yoga. And she does creative visualization meditation.

"My mom introduced me to that when I was really young. I was maybe about 12 or 13. Ever since then I have been meditating. I do a lot of yoga, as well, and I think that really helps me just have a balanced life," Andreescu said. "I don't only work on my physical aspect. I also work on the mental, because that's also very, very important. It's definitely showing through my matches where I'm staying in the present moment a lot of the time."

"I do creative visualization techniques in the morning. It's only 15 minutes. I used to do hours and hours of it, but I found that 15 minutes has really helped me, and it's not time-consuming at all," she added.

Andreescu also takes advantage of the services of a sports psychologist—something many players do, but most prefer not to discuss.

"I see her here and there. She's an amazing person. I can talk to her about anything. And she's very knowledgeable," Andreescu said.

8

A LIFE-CHANGING MOMENT

In that instant, when that final winning service return went past Serena Williams, Bianca Andreescu lifted her arms in triumph, her life instantly changed.

In the locker room afterward, a disappointed Williams made a point of coming up to her.

"She said some really nice things, which I'll cherish for a really, really long time," Andreescu said. "I've really strived to be like her. Who knows? Maybe I can be even better."

The hours immediately following the victory were filled with interviews with the various US Open television rights holders, and a well-attended press conference.

The 19-year-old walked into the room full of journalists and TV cameras with her poise still intact.

Well-known television broadcaster Mary Carillo asked perhaps the most pertinent question.

"How famous do you want to be? We can tell how good you want to be. Are you okay with the idea of being recognized all over the place? Was that all part of the dream?" she asked.

"I guess it is, yeah. I never really thought about being famous. My goals have been to just win as many Grand Slams as possible, become No. 1 in the world. But the idea of fame never really crossed my mind," Andreescu answered. "I'm not complaining,

Andreescu presents a replica "coach's trophy" to Sylvain Bruneau at her post-victory press conference.

though. It's been a crazy ride this year. I can definitely get used to this feeling."

She had been calm and cool throughout—until a seemingly anodyne moment when the full weight of her journey hit her.

Andreescu was talking about the visualization techniques that she has been using since she was a young teenager.

And it all came back to her—all the times she had imagined playing a Grand Slam final against Serena Williams.

"It's so crazy, man," she said, tears coming down her cheeks.

She took just a moment to compose herself, and went on.

"I've been dreaming of this moment for the longest time. After I won the (junior) Orange Bowl, a couple months after, I really believed that I could be at this stage. Since then, honestly, I've been visualizing it almost every single day," she added.

"For it to become a reality is just so crazy."

On Sunday morning, suited and booted, hair and makeup on point, Andreescu rode the elevators to the top of Rockefeller Center for the official champion's photo shoot.

The young woman on court in the purple-and-black Nike outfit worn by so many other players at the US Open was transformed into a glamorous champion in a black dress.

A full house in the main interview room at the US Open as Andreescu shares her post-victory thoughts.

Andreescu answered many of the same questions again. And she didn't seem to mind repeating herself in the least.

Her parents, Coco the dog, coach Sylvain Bruneau, agent Jonathan Dasnières de Veigy of Octagon, physical trainer Virginie Tremblay, physiotherapist Kirstin Bauer, and hitting partner Hugo di Feo all were on hand. The scenes were a little surreal.

That night, she watched her victory over Williams. "I usually don't like to watch myself play, but I'd only make the exception for that match," she said. "Just, wow. I still can't believe it."

Monday, she hit the New York talk-show circuit: *Live with Ryan and Kelly*, *Good Morning America*, *The View*, and *The Tonight Show Starring Jimmy Fallon*.

Andreescu was hoping to get in a little shopping on Fifth Ave. before leaving the city. But who had the time?

A Glorious Homecoming

Andreescu was whisked back to Toronto Tuesday afternoon in a private jet provided by an athlete empowerment brand founded by basketball legend LeBron James, which had just launched in Canada two months before.

There was a stunning bouquet of flowers. And some champagne. And the ride took just 45 minutes.

The perks of success were already looking pretty good.

First stop upon landing? A local shopping mall.

By Wednesday, another round of media commitments as her hometown celebrated her victory.

Congratulatory tweets from famous Canadian athletes and members of the NBA's Toronto Raptors. Messaging back and forth with Toronto-born rapper Drake.

And her own hashtag, #SheTheNorth, a takeoff on the championship Raptors' #WeTheNorth.

"I've had a lot of (celebrating). The last three days have been pretty bad for my diet. After the final, we had a really nice dinner in New York—just me and my team and my parents," Andreescu said. "Now that I'm home, I'm definitely going to celebrate with some of my friends, get to see them. But it's time to move on to the next after today."

Homegirl Goes Home

But first, a rally in her hometown of Mississauga, the Toronto suburb where she was born and raised until after she joined

Andreescu poses with her trophy at the top of Rockefeller Center in Manhattan.

Andreescu takes part in a homecoming rally in Mississauga. (Photo: AP Images)

Tennis Canada's national program, at which point the family moved to Vaughan—much closer to the tennis centre.

Thousands of people turned up as a street was renamed "Andreescu Way."

Even Canadian prime minister Justin Trudeau, on the campaign trail, showed up for hugs and congratulations.

The following Monday was named "Bianca Andreescu Day" in Toronto.

The new world No. 5 had entered tournaments in Japan and China immediately following the US Open. At the time, no one could have imagined that she would still be at Flushing Meadows on the final day.

Mindful of the heavy schedule that may have contributed to her summer shoulder woes, and needing the time to recover and—of course—get the promotional machine rolling, it was decided that she would withdraw from both events.

She then headed to Montreal for more public appearances and a week of solid training before jetting off to a top-level tournament in Beijing, China, well ahead of the event to acclimate to the jet lag.

"After Indian Wells it took a couple of weeks to sink in for that week. In Toronto, it took a couple of days. And now...I don't know how long it's going to take, but hopefully soon it can sink in," Andreescu said. "This is a Grand Slam. So I guess it's going to be different."

She arrived in Asia a star, with all eyes on her, after her star-making turn in New York.

Beijing was likely to be the penultimate tournament of an eventful season, with one more to go before a well-earned vacation.

The 2019 season was coming to a close.

But Andreescu's journey was just beginning. ●

Parents Maria and Nicu and the other new star, toy poodle Coco, joined Andreescu for the champion's official photo shoot.

COCO ANDREESCU IS A STAR

There have been some legendary dogs in WTA Tour history, going back to Roland (Arantxa Sanchez Vicario's Pomeranian, named after her victory at Roland Garros) and K.D. (short for "Killer Dog," exactly what Martina Navratilova's toy fox terrier was not).

Always classics are Christopher Chip Rafael Nadal Williams (Serena's Yorkshire Terrier, "Chip" for short) and Harry Reginald Williams (Venus' Havanese, "Harry" for short).

But Coco Andreescu, US Open champion Bianca Andreescu's caramel-colored toy poodle, got nearly as much attention as the champion herself at the 2019 US Open.

Coco came into the Andreescus' lives in May 2018, a month after they lost their beloved Jessica.

She made her big-league debut at the Miami Open back in March, where she would lie under the hot metal seats chewing on a bone, oblivious to everything around her.

By the Rogers Cup in Toronto, everyone knew who she was.

By the US Open, she was a star. Dogs aren't allowed in the seats at the US Open, but the Andreescus were able to bring Coco in, and put her under the seat and out of sight.

After Andreescu's victory, she was asked about the first purchase she would make with the winner's check for $3.85 million.

"She's getting her own Coco Chanel collar. Hell yeah! She deserves it," Andreescu said.

9

WHAT'S NEXT?

Where does Bianca Andreescu go from here?

Well, there are still so many mountains to climb, goals to reach.

She's just getting started.

After the US Open win, Andreescu said she wanted to qualify for the year-end WTA finals in Shenzhen, China, in late October.

That goal was accomplished in Beijing, where she returned to action at the China Open three weeks after winning the title in New York.

Andreescu picked up right where she had left off in New York—until she faced Japan's Naomi Osaka in a highly anticipated meeting in the quarterfinal.

Osaka, her predecessor as US Open champion, won the dramatic encounter 5-7, 6-3, 6-4—and won the tournament.

It was the first meeting between the two young stars, and it definitely set the stage for a friendly but intense rivalry over the next decade.

Andreescu was also aiming to finish in the top three in the 2019 year-end rankings, which certainly was in reach if she did well in the final competition of the season.

After what surely will feel like an extremely short off-season break, Andreescu will soon be back preparing for 2020.

She will kick off her year where it all began back in January, at the ASB Classic in Auckland, New Zealand. From there she'll head for the Australian Open, where she will be among the favorites to back up her first Grand Slam title with a second one.

It wouldn't be unprecedented. In fact, it happened very recently.

Andreescu returned to the court three weeks later in Beijing, where she met Japanese star Naomi Osaka for the first time, in the quarterfinal. Theirs could be a gripping rivalry over the next decade. (Photo: AP Images)

In 2018, Osaka was ranked No. 44 going into the BNP Paribas Open in March. A true longshot, the 20-year-old won the Indian Wells title.

At the US Open later that year, Osaka defeated Serena Williams to win her first Grand Slam title. And in Australia the following January, now ranked No. 4, she won her second major and became the No. 1 player in the world.

The challenge for Andreescu, as it was with Osaka, will be to deal with the reality that almost every aspect of her life has changed overnight.

Andreescu had already earned more than $6 million on the court through the 2019 US Open—a life-changing amount of money.

And she appears set to earn a significant amount off the court as well, as her agents look to secure new sponsors and long-term partnerships.

There will be more demands on her time, between media requests and commitments to sponsors and a growing fan base.

Most of all, she will have to continue to develop her game.

Andreescu burst onto the scene in Auckland with little fanfare. She was the hunter, and some of the best players in the world didn't know what hit them.

Until the loss to Osaka in Beijing, she had won all eight of her matches against top-10 players in 2019.

In 2020, she will be one of the best players in the world. And the rest of the women on the WTA Tour will redouble their efforts to scout her, figure out her game, pinpoint any weaknesses, and try to find a way to beat her.

Andreescu can ask Serena Williams all about that. She has been the hunted for nearly two decades, and has fended off most all of her challengers through the years.

And there will be ranking points to defend, which immediately adds additional pressure.

It is a peculiarity of the tennis ranking system, which is calculated on a 52-week rolling basis, that to stay in place, you must do at least as well as you did the previous year.

To move up—in Andreescu's case, to aspire to be No. 1—you must do even better.

Above all, Andreescu must continue to focus on staying as healthy as a player can, given the length of the season.

She has a lot to look forward to, as she missed nearly the entirety of the spring clay-court swing and the summer grass-court campaign in 2019 with her shoulder injury.

On those natural surfaces, Andreescu's creative game can thrive just as well, or better, as they did on the hard courts in New York. But to take advantage, she will have to remain healthy during the entire season.

If she does, the sky could well be the limit.

And from the very first strike of the ball in Auckland, she'll have an entire nation of new fans cheering her on. ●

Now that she's a Grand Slam champion, every move Andreescu makes will be scrutinized by the media and all of her new fans.